Children, Art, Artists

Centro internazionale per la difesa e la promozione
dei diritti e delle potenzialità dei bambini e delle bambine

Children, Art, Artists
The expressive languages of children,
the artistic language of Alberto Burri

© 2004 Preschools and Infant-toddler Centers
Istituzione of the Municipality of Reggio Emilia

February 2004 (1st edition)

Images on page 130-132
© Fondazione Palazzo Albizzini Collezione Burri, Città di Castello

ISBN 88-87960-38-0

published by:

REGGIO CHIDREN srl
Registered office: Via Guido da Castello, 12
Operative office: Piazza della Vittoria, 6 - 42100 Reggio Emilia - Italy
tel. +39 0522 455416   fax +39 0522 455621
e-mail info@reggiochildren.it
website: www.reggiochildren.it

Cod. Fisc. e P.IVA 01586410357 - Cap. Soc. Euro 260.000,00
Iscr. al Reg. Impr. di Reggio E. n. 01586410357 - REA n. 197516

Children, Art, Artists

The expressive languages of children,
the artistic language of Alberto Burri

the didactic project

**The expressive languages of children,
the artistic language of Alberto Burri**
October 2001 – January 2002

Promoted by the Civic Museums, Reggio Children, the
Documentation and Educational Research Center, ReMida

Project director
Vea Vecchi, consultant to Reggio Children

Civic Museums of Reggio Emilia, coordination
Elisabetta Farioli, Assistant Director of the Civic Museums

Reggio Children, coordination
Claudia Giudici, pedagogista
Vea Vecchi, atelierista

Documentation and Educational Research Center (CDRE),
Istituzione of the Municipality of Reggio Emilia, coordination
Tiziana Filippini, pedagogista
Mirella Ruozzi, atelierista

ReMida, coordination
Elena Giacopini, pedagogista
Graziella Brighenti, organizational coordinator

Coordinators of the projects carried out with the children
Luigi Bellelli Infant-toddler Center - Lucia Colla, Lorena Lucenti, Mirella
Ruozzi, Tiziana Filippini, Claudia Giudici, Barbara Fabbi, Marina Ferrari,
Emanuela Paglia
Panda Infant-toddler Center – Lorena Lucenti, Lucia Colla, Mirella Ruozzi,
Tiziana Filippini, Claudia Giudici, Monica Borsini, Morgana Giberti
Ernesto Balducci Preschool – Mirca Neroni, Antonio Tinti, Daniela Chioffi,
Daniela Lanzi, Mirella Ruozzi
Choreia Preschool – Barbara Pini, Francesca Bianchi, Paola Cavazzoni
Diana Preschool – Isabella Meninno, Marina Mori, Evelina Reverberi,
Laura Rubizzi, Tiziana Filippini, Mariangela Bendusi, Lorena Chiessi,
Sonia Cipolla, Sandra Mercati, Paola Strozzi, Vea Vecchi
Iqbal Masih Preschool – Consuelo Damasi, Riccarda Bedini,
Daniela Lanzi, Elisabetta De Santi, Lorena Prandi
Bruno Munari Preschool – Barbara Quinti, Claudia Giudici, Elena Corte
Gianni Rodari Preschool (Sant'Ilario) – Filippo Chieli, Elena Maccaferri,
Paola Rubertelli, Sandra Garimberti, Lorella Trancossi
Giovanni Fiastri Preschool (Sant'Ilario) – Filippo Chieli, Elena Maccaferri,
Fausta Benassi, Maria De Biase, Lorella Trancossi
Annunziata Bergonzi Elementary School – Maria Grazia Stefanini,
Mirella Ruozzi, Lorella Prandi, Vania Zannoni
Don Pasquino Borghi Middle School – Sonia Benevelli

Expressive workshops, coordination:
Ines Bertolini, Elisabetta Farioli, Vea Vecchi
Workshops conducted by: Rossana Bianchini, Sara Bompani,
Giorgia Cantoni, Renza Grossi, Sabina Lugli, Roberta Pedroni

the exhibit

**The expressive languages of children,
the artistic language of Alberto Burri**
November 16 – December 8, 2002

Promoted by
Municipality of Reggio Emilia
Infant-toddler Centers and Preschools*
Civic Museums
Documentation and Educational Research Center
Reggio Children

with the contribution of Coopsette and ReMida

Exhibit design and organization
Tiziana Filippini, Claudia Giudici, Isabella Meninno, Mirella Ruozzi,
Vea Vecchi

Photographs, slides, and videos
Fausta Benassi, Claudio Cigarini, Filippo Chieli, Consuelo Damasi,
Alba Ferrari, Marina Ferrari, Penny Lawrence, Lorena Lucenti,
Elena Maccaferri, Isabella Meninno, Marina Mori, Mirca Neroni,
Barbara Pini, Barbara Quinti, Mirella Ruozzi, Andrea Zamboni

*since September 2003
Preschools and Infant-toddler Centers – Istituzione of the
Municipality of Reggio Emilia

the book

Children, Art, Artists
The expressive languages of children,
the artistic language of Alberto Burri

edited by — Vea Vecchi and Claudia Giudici

texts by — Filippo Chieli, Daniela Chioffi, Lucia Colla, Consuelo Damasi, Tiziana Filippini, Claudia Giudici, Renza Grossi, Lorena Lucenti, Elena Maccaferri, Isabella Meninno, Marina Mori, Mirca Neroni, Barbara Pini, Lorella Prandi, Barbara Quinti, Evelina Reverberi, Laura Rubizzi, Mirella Ruozzi, Mariagrazia Stefanini, Antonio Tinti, Lorella Trancossi, Vea Vecchi

contributions by — Enrico Banfi, Sandra Piccinini

and by — Paola Cavazzoni, Lucia Colla, Daniela Lanzi, Laura Rubizzi, Mirella Ruozzi, Antonio Tinti

photographs by — Fausta Benassi, Marina Castagnetti, Filippo Chieli, Consuelo Damasi, Barbara Fabbi, Marina Ferrari, Lorena Lucenti, Elena Maccaferri, Isabella Meninno, Marina Mori, Mirca Neroni, Barbara Pini, Barbara Quinti, Mirella Ruozzi, Antonio Tinti

and by — Claudio Cigarini, Alba Ferrari, Andrea Zamboni

concept and graphic design — Rolando Baldini, Vania Vecchi

page layout — Rolando Baldini

publishing coordinators — Claudia Giudici and Annamaria Mucchi

English translation — Gabriella Grasselli and Leslie Morrow

on the cover — *Pulvirized recomposed*, Clara, anni 4,7
photographs by Isabella Meninno and Mirca Neroni

printed by — Grafiche Rebecchi Ceccarelli - Cognento (Modena)

Special thanks to the following for their invaluable contribution: Chiara Sarteanesi (Palazzo Albizzini Collezione Burri Foundation, Città di Castello), Marina Castagnetti and Fabio Lucenti (Documentation and Educational Research Center, Istituzione of the Municipality of Reggio Emilia)

The city, the children, and contemporary art:
A cultural project extending beyond the exhibit

Sandra Piccinini
President of the Preschools and Infant-toddler Centers Istituzione
of the Municipality of Reggio Emilia, at the time of the project
Commissioner of Culture and Education of the Municipality of Reggio Emilia

The Alberto Burri exhibit was held in Reggio Emilia in November 2001 at the Cloisters of San Domenico as a collateral event to an important restoration project on the old coach terminal, commonly known in the town as Sarsa.

The initiative took shape thanks to a collaborative effort between the Civic Museums, the Albizzini Foundation of Città di Castello, and a group of businesses (Coopsette, Esselunga, and ACI), with the aim to organize an important cultural event as part of the inauguration of the space, which had been painstakingly restored and would be used for new purposes in the future.

The city of Reggio Emilia provided a favorable and receptive context for the Alberto Burri exhibit, because our city has always been attentive to the new and over the years has consistently promoted contemporary culture, keeping in tune with the spirit of the times. Since the 1960s, in fact, Reggio Emilia has been a place where avant-garde culture has been experimented and consolidated. Our city has hosted avant-garde artists from every field, in a vision of art that is not based on specialism. For instance, Living Theatre made Reggio Emilia its Italian home, and equally at home here was the musical experimentation of Claudio Abbado, Maurizio Pollini, and Salvatore Sciarrino. This is just to mention a few of the important names in contemporary music who, as young and still unknown artists, performed in our neighborhoods and factories as part of an experience called "Music and Reality." On the occasion of the Alberto Burri exhibit, we felt the need to go beyond the single event, because today it is not so important to organize large-scale episodic events, but to invest in that which sediments culture and knowledge, especially in times like ours where memory is short-lived.

It was certainly not the first experience in which our schools and children encountered important cultural opportunities in the town. It would suffice to recall the children's creation of a house curtain for the Ariosto Theater, but also a more short-term project like "Duemila Anni Luce" (Two Thousand Light Years). In this project, to highlight the Galleria Parmeggiani (an important art museum in the town), the collection of old art works was displayed together with works by contemporary artists, and the children of the Diana preschool made their own contribution with a work made of light! Alongside the Burri exhibit, we thus organized a special project for the schools based on a collaboration between the Municipal Infant-toddler Centers and Preschools, Reggio Children, and ReMida (the recycling center that collects unused materials from industry to give them new life through creative processes).

The events related to the Burri exhibit actually began prior to its inauguration, with a preview in the form of a visit to the Albizzini Foundation in Città di Castello by a large group of teachers; and the project continued in the schools (infant-toddler centers, preschools, elementary and middle schools) after the exhibit closed.

One year later, another exhibit was held, showing works made by children in the schools and in the expressive workshops. These works are presented here in this book, the result of an intelligent project of professional development and enthusiasm, the echoes of which we have continued to hear. My personal appreciation and thanks, along with those of a city that knows it can be proud of this enthusiasm, passion, and intelligence, go to everyone involved in the project.

Following this experience, another exhibit lent itself to an encounter with the children. "Alfabeto in sogno" (Alphabet in Dreams) dealt with the theme of figurative poetry, using old, modern, and contemporary manuscripts and prints to document how words take on "substance and image" through poetry and writing.

These are just a few examples to illustrate how we have conceived cultural exhibits in the town ("Duemila Anni Luce", "Alberto Burri", "Alfabeto in Sogno") as a special opportunity for us and the children to reflect on and re-think about their communicative expressiveness through words (written and spoken), and through materials and their various languages.

Currently, an even more ambitious project is in progress: "Invito a…" (Invitation to…), an invitation to artists of our times to revisit places in the city that in the last few years have undergone restoration or have been given new uses, places that will be transformed through the artists' interpretations.

Sol LeWitt, Richard Serra, and Lucio Fabro are just a few of the artists who have accepted the invitation and will establish genuine cultural work sites in the city. Here, too, we will seek an ongoing dialogue with the children who, like artists, have a different way of seeing things.

It is an invitation to design permanent works of art in a city that will itself become an art gallery, in line with the contemporary idea of the city as a large museum. The experiment has already begun, guided by Claudio Parmigiani (artist and project curator), with whom we have reopened an old church in the town center that had been closed for more than fifty years. Will the city rediscovered and re-seen through the eyes of contemporary artists become aesthetically more appreciable? This is what is needed in our times.

The aim of these concrete actions by the Municipality is to ensure that the city remains in keeping with the spirit of our times, and reflects the contemporary world, obviously without repudiating the characteristics peculiar to identity that have always made ours a city that knows how to do things and how to live.

Like many European cities, Reggio Emilia is going through a crucial period of transition between what it was and what it can become, with the potential risk of remaining suspended between a certain nostalgia for the past (provincial but more reassuring) and the fear of imagining itself as a dynamic, multiethnic city in the future. This future is already being written in the everyday lives of many local families, if it is true that 14% of the children in our town have one parent who comes from outside Italy, and an equal percentage of families are "mixed."

What should be the goal of the cultural initiatives of a municipality that seeks to encourage the projection of its community into the future rather than its static preservation or retrogression?

To encourage cultural production, to encourage the encounter between different kinds of knowledge that are not separated, between scientific and humanistic culture, for instance; not to separate school and culture, because schools produce culture daily, when they manage to find the energy to be creative rather than repetitive.

Focusing on culture as the field of action for the development of cities is a choice made by a number of important European cities. Reggio Emilia is thus carrying out its own "trials of the future," in the knowledge that we can count on an extraordinary ability to get things done and on the strength of so much collective intelligence.

Today, Reggio Emilia is trying to imagine its future, knowing that we are often capable of realizing the improbable.

A Guide for the Reader

This catalogue is designed to offer a "guided tour" of the exhibit entitled "The Expressive Languages of Children, the Artistic Language of Alberto Burri," which included works by children ranging in age from the infant-toddler center to the elementary school.

We decided to publish the materials as they were presented in the exhibit, with the addition of a few general reflections as an introduction to each project and brief comments during the project descriptions where it seemed necessary in order to clarify the documentation displayed and to examine it in more depth. Along with the texts of the exhibit, the catalogue includes a number of essays discussing the relationship between schools and the city, children and art, and pedagogy and the atelier.

We feel that this structure will make it possible to talk about the ideas presented in the exhibit in different places and contexts, communicating an approach of children to art and artists that we feel is interesting for the world of schools and the world of museums, enabling an exchange of different points of view.

These choices were made to ensure that the catalogue would be consistent with the overall project, which was primarily a project of professional formation and development for teachers and atelieristas (from the infant-toddler center through middle school), on a theme that is delicate, important, and necessary: the encounter between children and the poetic languages. We feel that this dialogue can promote a kind of knowledge that is more human and more complete.

note

to distinguish the text that accompanied the exhibit from the comments added subsequently in the catalogue, **this typeface has been used.**

the professional development project

The professional development project was promoted and coordinated by Reggio Children, the Central Administration of the Municipal Infant-toddler Centers and Preschools, the Documentation and Educational Research Center, the Civic Museums, and the ReMida Creative Recycling Center.

1. In October 2001, a large group of atelieristas and teachers from the infant-toddler centers, preschools, elementary and middle schools, along with personnel from the Civic Museums of Reggio Emilia, traveled to Città di Castello to view works by artist Alberto Burri at the Albizzini Foundation. The visit was guided by Chiara Sarteanesi, curator of the foundation's collection.

2. A three-day workshop was held at ReMida (see profile on page 154), which included both theoretical sessions and hands-on exploration of materials. This experience enabled the participants to reflect together on the works by Burri they had seen and to select a number of characteristics that could be the focus of interesting projects to work on with the children. From Burri's works, the features chosen for this focus included: the use of materials as pictorial coloring, "listening" to the identity of the single materials, the variation and transformation of the material, and the compositional strategies.

One aspect that was consistently underscored was the need, in working with the children, to avoid any formal copying of the works of Burri and, rather, to grasp their poetic suggestions for approaching things.

The aim was to propose these approaches to the children in tune with their own autonomous strategies, observing and documenting as thoroughly as possible the paths taken by the children individually and in groups.

3. Thus began the work with children in the different schools (the project lasted from one to three months).

4. The Alberto Burri exhibit was inaugurated in Reggio Emilia.

5. Chiara Sarteanesi held a public conference to present and comment on Burri's works for the benefit of teachers. A copy of the exhibit catalogue was given to each participant.

6. During the entire period in which the exhibit was shown, the museum conducted expressive workshops for groups of students from preschool to middle school age as the initial phase of introduction to the exhibit. Subsequently, the children were taken to visit the Burri exhibit.

7. Atelieristas and teachers produced slide documentaries narrating the work carried out in each infant-toddler center and school. While the documentaries were being edited, two work sessions were organized to present them to a larger group of teachers, atelieristas, and pedagogistas for their critiques.

8. The documentation of the children's work was presented by the atelieristas and teachers themselves in the exhibit "The Expressive Languages of Children, the Artistic Language of Alberto Burri," shown at the local museum. In the experience of producing this instrument of communication, many atelieristas and teachers learned for the first time how to use certain digital technologies.

The project involved children and teachers from the infant-toddler center through middle school. Viewing Burri's works suggested to the teachers certain approaches and concepts regarding materials, which they tailored appropriately to propose to their students:
the identity of the material investigated
chromatic identity (painting with material)
compositional rigor
variation (tactile, perceptual, compositional)
transformability
intensity in the way of looking at everyday things.

The children explored the material, dialoguing with it, "painted" with the material, created compositions, and only afterward visited the Burri exhibit, where they observed and commented on the works.

9. Throughout the period of the exhibit (from November 16 to December 8, 2002), evening slide presentations and guided tours were organized for the families of the children of the infant-toddler centers, preschools, and elementary schools.

10. In March 2002, the exhibit "The Expressive Languages of Children, the Artistic Language of Alberto Burri" was shown in the nearby town of Sant'Ilario in the province of Reggio Emilia.

11. The catalogue of the exhibit that you have in your hands became a further instrument of communication about the work carried out.

12. The project as a whole provided material for professional development initiatives with teachers and museum personnel in Italy and abroad.

Poster of the Alberto Burri exhibit

Poster of the exhibit of projects carried out with the children

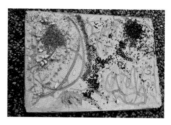

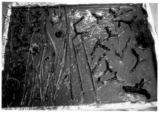

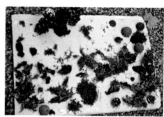

Slabs of scagliola form an extraordinary path that has captured the gestures, materials, and imagination of children at the infant-toddler center, and marks the entrance to the exhibit "The Expressive Languages of Children, the Artistic Language of Alberto Burri."

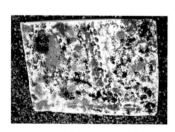

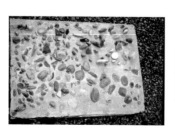

"The road of wonders"
authors: children from 18 to 32 months old at the Bellelli infant-toddler center

The project

The expressive languages of children,
the artistic language of Alberto Burri

The intrinsic structure of the expressive languages is such that they are able to maintain a strong connection between rationality and imagination, cognitivity and sensitivity. They thus become the most effective antibodies to violence and the most conducive means for listening to others and the world.

Like other expressive languages, the visual language is a gift that belongs to every man and woman right from birth, and it evolves and is nurtured by favorable cultural contexts.

The works of artists offer food for thought and for the imagination, but in working with children the primary focus is, and must always remain, the children themselves, with their own strategies of thought, their knowledge-building processes, and their relationships.

So what we need to seek out and apply when working with the children are some of the processes involved in the creative act, such as synthesis, exploratory tension, the intense relationship with things, symbolic invention, metaphor, evocation and analogy, cultural courage, and expressivity.

The teacher's role is to be a competent listener to the visual language and to the children's individual and group strategies in order to support the children in a way that is in tune with their autonomous expression.

Luigi Bellelli Infant-toddler Center
2001-2002 school year

Project coordinators
Lucia Colla
Lorena Lucenti
Mirella Ruozzi
Tiziana Filippini
Claudia Giudici

Barbara Fabbi
Marina Ferrari
Emanuela Paglia

Texts
Lucia Colla
Lorena Lucenti
Mirella Ruozzi

Photographs
Mirella Ruozzi
Marina Ferrari
Barbara Fabbi

Authors
children from 7 to 28 months old

Panda Infant-toddler Center
2001-2002 school year

Project coordinators
Lorena Lucenti
Lucia Colla
Mirella Ruozzi
Tiziana Filippini
Claudia Giudici

Monica Borsini
Morgana Giberti

Texts
Lucia Colla
Lorena Lucenti
Mirella Ruozzi

Photographs
Lorena Lucenti
Mirella Ruozzi

Authors
children from 8 to 37 months old

View of the "Whites and Blacks" section

black is made
of all the colors/
it's all whites

Black is made of all the colors / It's all whites

The project that developed around the Burri exhibit in Reggio Emilia was an opportunity not only for more in-depth examination and research on the children's expressive languages but also for us, as teachers at the infant-toddler center, to build new cultural and pedagogical knowledge. Prior to this experience, we had often made use of the ateliers of the preschools to mediate our work on cultural and artistic themes, but we had rarely dialogued directly with the conceptual aspects of artistic culture.

Our intention was not only to keep a trace of the children's actions and gestures and give them appropriate visibility, but also to improve our own ability to see and define the qualities and peculiarities of the children's explorations.

It was not easy to find knowledge-building strategies that would dialogue with the artistic experience and work of Alberto Burri, or to develop, with the necessary sensitivity and respect (for the children and for the artist), possible paths to explore with the children.

We introduced some contexts for studying the materials; subsequently, with more conscious and demanding thoughts, we designed contexts for the research to be carried out with the children and selected the materials to propose to them.

Thinking about the "material"* characteristics of the materials we had chosen led to broader reflections; for example, regarding the choices we make as teachers each time we identify possible materials to use at the infant-toddler center.

From a very young age, children demonstrate their fascination with the search for the essence of things; how aware are we of their daily encounters not only with objects but also with their constituent materials?

The children's way of looking helped us to put this question into focus and to construct new awarenesses and understandings about their curiosities and knowledge-building processes.

In both infant-toddler centers, we worked with the infants' group (6-10 months) and the Toddlers 2 group (18-24 months), choosing the material and its variations: different types of plastic, paper, fabric.

We also chose to explore white and black monochromatically, because the children consistently show us how capable they are of perceiving even the smallest chromatic nuances, as well as tactile, auditory, and olfactory differences.

The choice of these two colors, white for Bellelli and black for Panda, was not random. For different reasons, it was a sort of provocative declaration, because both of these colors are generally not considered colors at all and are rarely considered in terms of their different shades.

In Western society, white symbolizes purity, innocence, morality, rigor. Black, on the other hand, is seen as the color of darkness, fear, and mourning, and is almost never associated with young children or thought of as a color for them.

Having made this bold decision, our impression was that the children approached white and black alike with equal curiosity; in fact, they defined both colors as beautiful and recognized their range of shades:

There are black blacks and there are more colored blacks, says Carolina (32 months).

They're whites; they're not all the same, says Eva (24 months).

* Translators' note: In Italian the word "materico" is an adjective form of the noun "materia," which means "matter" (differently from "materiale," which is "material" as both adjective and noun). Since this form does not exist in English, here and throughout the book we have used "material" as an adjective to convey this meaning.

blacks and whites

Considering how important the floor is for children of this age, since it is one of the surfaces they most frequently inhabit, we offered the children in the infants' group at Panda a large carpet of different materials in shades of black, and in the same group at Bellelli a large carpet of different materials in shades of white, along with a path made of white materials with different sonorous possibilities.

Before proposing these contexts to the children, however, the teachers made hypotheses and shared ideas about how to design them. We spent a good deal of time putting together, preparing, and evaluating the materials and their qualities (also aesthetic), and deciding how far apart from each other or close together the different materials should be on the carpet.

The idea was to offer the children a large surface to explore that would, along with initially creating surprise, take into account their knowledge-building rhythms and strategies.

View of work from the Bellelli and Panda infant-toddler centers

"The true depth of the beauty of white and black is revealed only to those eyes that are able to appreciate the splendor of colors that are sumptuous and vivid, with all their gradations and nuances."
from *Il sentimento del colore*, Quaderni di Eranos

black is made of all the colors Federica, 32 months

multisensory landscapes

Carpet of blacks proposed to the children

What elements can establish a relationship between children from eight months to two years old and a mature and famous artist like Alberto Burri?

Perhaps one is a way of looking at the world around you that is not yet enclosed in rigid categories of thought. Another could be the pleasure of understanding things also by using your hands.

The enchantment of having a perceptual competence that enables you to grasp chromatic gradations. Exploring with all your senses to create a relationship with the world around you.

A way of looking that makes everyday things special.

it's all whites Elisa, 25 months

multisensory landscapes

Che cosa
relazione
mesi ai du
maturo e f
Burri?

Forse uno
che ci circ
racchiuso
pensiero r
forse il pia
attraverso
Una comp
incantata
le gradazio
tutti i sensi
entrare in
mondo.
Uno sguar
speciali gli
quotidianità.

**è tut
bian**

**paesaggi
polisensor**

progetto
realizzato
con i bambini
dagli 8 ai 22 mes

Carpet of whites proposed to the children

material gradations of whites and blacks

On the two large carpets, the children immediately perceived the threshold, a sort of boundary line full of expectations and curiosities that drew them cautiously into this sort of new monochromatic landscape, sometimes just touching the surface.

The children used their bodies to establish a relationship with the material, changing and modifying their postures in order to better investigate it, but also immersing themselves to encounter the materials and explore their diversities.

With their bodies, the children discovered, twisted, explored, and transformed, sometimes reducing the boundary lines and sometimes creating other, unexpected ones. Torn or rolled up bits in the materials caused the children to stumble and sometimes temporarily withdraw from the carpet, while at other times this stimulated new encounters and curiosities.

The children investigated this place-landscape with every part of their bodies: eyes, hands, and feet became sensitive receptors that clearly listened to and explored the material and its perceptual, visual, and sonorous qualities.

Sonority. The children shook, struck, plucked, and pounded to hear rhythmic and sonorous qualities; they became quiet with the materials that made sounds and "talked" to the silent ones.

Tactility. The children stroked the materials to feel their tactile qualities: smooth, rough, flat, satiny, puckered, wrinkled. They pressed and crumpled, rolled and unrolled, pulled and released, to test the consistency, the softness, the hardness, the rigidity of the materials; to see how the material retained traces-proof of their actions.

The children who were already walking traversed the entire surface, experimenting with a sort of dance-exploration in which the rhythm of the movement was marked by the different tactile perceptions "listened to" by feet that are sensitive and intelligent.

Smell and taste. The children also explored the materials by tasting them and sniffing them to smell their odors.

Each child used his or her own strategy to approach the material.

For all the children, the time spent exploring was long, almost expanded, in what seemed to us to be the alternating rhythms of learning: nearing and distancing, entering and exiting, pausing and accelerating.

View of work from the Bellelli and Panda infant-toddler centers

The children's explorations were intense, concentrated, aimed at penetrating the essence of the material.

Their hands rubbed, balled up, bent, rolled, crumpled, tore, transformed.

They tested the reversibility and conservation of the qualities of the material.

The way in which they aligned, overlapped, brought together, and rearranged the materials seemed to show the genesis of composition.

exploratory experiments

With the Toddlers 2 groups, the exploration of the material involved creating a collection of black and white materials, chosen with the children's help.

Paper, fabric, and plastic, white and black, were chosen for their variations in texture, weight, size, bulk, consistency, transparency, and elasticity.

Like the younger children, the toddlers showed individual methods and strategies for getting to know the material, but they also devoted a great deal of attention to the gestures of the other children in their research.

This created a fertile and interesting atmosphere of group work, where the presence of others was necessary for learning and understanding. The children's ways of exploring differed. Some of them proceeded by analogy,

choosing materials based on similar characteristics; for example, types of paper that tear more easily, plastics that retain an imprint longer. Others proceeded by differences; for example, using the gestures of wrapping packages, two girls alternated thin paper with heavier paper.

Some children seemed to evaluate the characteristics of the materials at first glance, as if they did not need to touch them. A lightweight piece of paper evoked the idea of flight and the children, looking at all the types of paper and choosing with precision, tried out the one that flew the best. Other children perceived the potentials of the material in terms of tactile variations, so in their exploration, corrugated cardboard seemed to become a piano keyboard that they played with knowing and refined gestures.

I'm making a present of whites; it's a present all inside!
Eva, 24 months

There are black blacks,
and blacks that are more colored.
Carolina, 32 months

Genesis of composition

In these explorations of matter and material, there seemed to be the genesis of composition, or perhaps a compositional research already in place, with its own strategies and aims. This research involved all the sensory approaches that characterized the children's explorations of the single materials.

Some children chose materials (in this case, fabrics) to compose on the table top, first putting them up to their faces, as if to confirm the sensitivity of their cheeks.

Other children, after choosing the materials, arranged them close together, and the composition was formed through a narration that created a relationship between them.

For example, Giulia, after having explored some pieces of black fabric, said: *It closes everything*, enclosing the pieces of fabric within a perimeter of little strips of white fabric.

The compositional research was sometimes symmetrical, sometimes random, sometimes unexpected, often aesthetically beautiful, as the children themselves said: *I like it the way I put it like that; otherwise it wouldn't be pretty!* (Eva, 24 months)

Sara, 21 months

Iuri, 21 months

Compositions

Linda, 37 months

Iris, 20 months

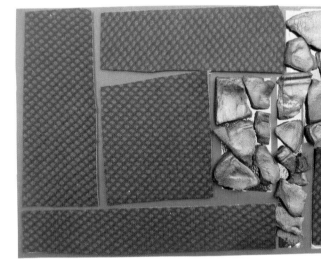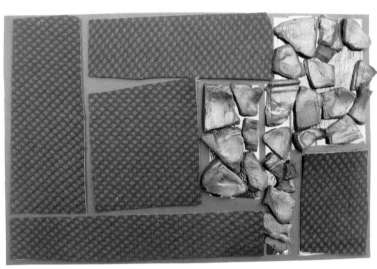

Michele, 26 months

Queenly Nana, 36 months

Alessandra, 26 months

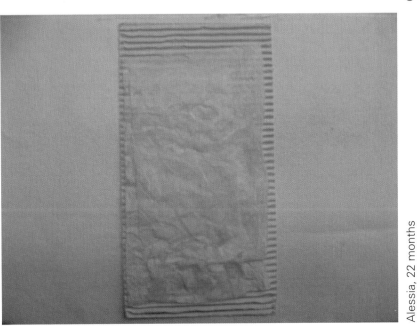

Alessia, 22 months

Diana Preschool
2001-2002 school year

Project coordinators
Isabella Meninno
Marina Mori
Tiziana Filippini
Vea Vecchi

Mariangela Benedusi
Lorena Chiessi

Texts
Isabella Meninno
Marina Mori
Vea Vecchi

Photographs
Isabella Meninno
Marina Mori

Authors
three- and four-year-old children

View of work from the Diana preschool

white, white, and white

Exhibit of work from the Diana preschool

White, white, and white Alberto, 3 yrs.

A paper napkin on a table. An object that is camouflaged by normal use and everyday-ness, in some way becoming anonymous. An object we have already assimilated, already experienced. A "habitual material" which, when observed with searching eyes, eyes that distinguish, can become something else: white, airy, and delicate; just a bit rough; overlaid and opaque; or open and almost transparent.

A napkin removed from invisibility and made the protagonist of attentions and reflections.

From the object-napkin function, we change direction and are catapulted into the discovery of the known-unknown paper napkin, making it something special because we look at it in a special way.

As hands, brain, sensations, and material got to know each other, the children's gestures constructed the first forms: folding, wrinkling, rolling up, crumpling, pulling, and tearing the material, and inventing suitable words to describe it.

These first forms embodied alphabets, the search for a material grammar that became richer and more complex by exploring fabrics, plastic, and paper in different shades of white; other softnesses, roughnesses, forms, mental images, other material alphabets, leading to the construction of small compositions using these materials.

Combinations, alliances, dialogues of materials; perceptual, pictorial, and material solutions with chromatic, formal, and compositional variations.

The final compositions were the result of agreements reached, a sort of pact of alliance between the children and the material. Each composition bore the personal traces, thoughts, and imprints of the children and the quality, identity, and peculiarity of the materials.

When these compositions were combined, they integrated each other, confronted each other, and were expanded to be recombined again in other compositions.

A recombination that searched for equilibrium with other gestures and other thoughts: recombining means re-seeing, re-listening, re-imagining.

It was a process of becoming that ended only when the "compositional tuning" was complete.

A large final composition gave the children a sense of the dimensions of the work they had done.

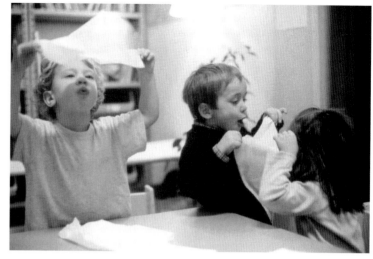

it smells good
you can tear it
it puffs up
soft white
like a rug
soft like a cat's tail
it flies up when you blow on it
it's special

a paper napkin that's special

An anonymous object, camouflaged by normal use and everyday-ness, becomes special when you look at it in a special way.

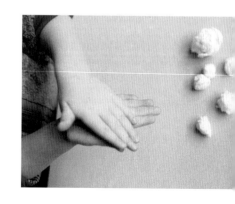

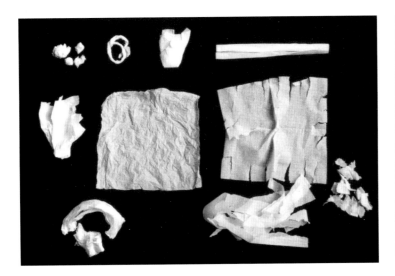 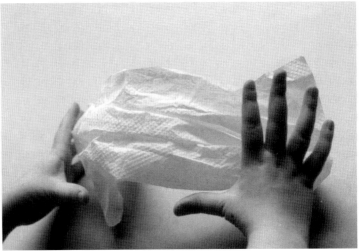

alphabets of gestures, forms, mental images

balling up, folding, wrinkling, modeling, pulling, making hoods

I'm tearing off a piece of paper and I'm making it a hood. Lorenzo, 3 yrs. 5 mos.

In contact with the children's hands, the material underwent yet another transformation. These were the first gestures, the first forms.
We made a sort of catalogue of them.
The children experimented with resistance, lightness, and delicacy; it was often the material itself, reluctant to be modified, that surprised them.

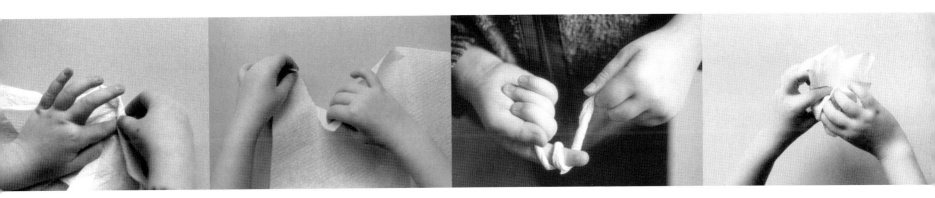

In transforming the napkin, the children alternated between abstract perceptions and figurative images, both legitimate and interesting.

it's a snake

Giovanni, 3 yrs.

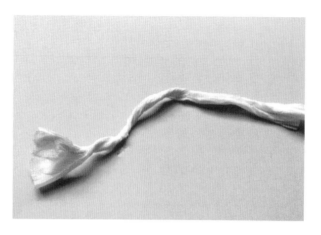

now it's a crocodile. . .

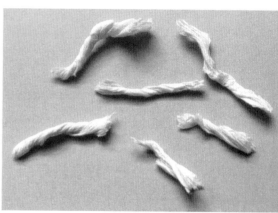

they're sharks

The children "navigated" from one image to another, from one analogy to another, from one abstraction to another. A snake was transformed into a crocodile, the crocodile into a school of scary sharks, and suddenly a napkin on your head made witches and wizards appear.

Word, gesture, and mental image were three mutually nurturing elements of an indissoluble relationship. Words followed gestures, which followed words, which followed images, which followed gestures, which followed words...

first compositions

We suggested that the children keep their transformations of the napkin by gluing them, as they liked, onto one of the bases that we proposed: square pieces of paper of the same size as the original napkin in different shades of white, black, and gray.

I put them on the white one because it (the napkin) *wanted the white.* Alberto A., 3 yrs. 1 mo.

I put them here (black base) *because otherwise they don't work* (you can't see them well). Riccardo, 3 yrs. 9 mos.

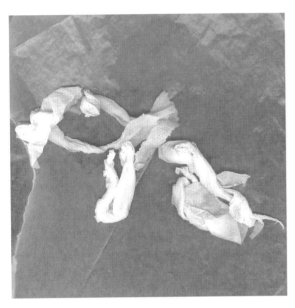

Luca B., 3 yrs. 5 mos.

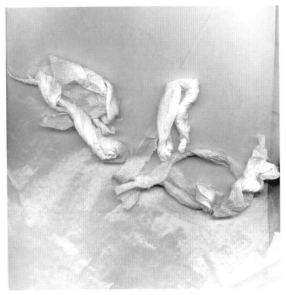

Cecilia, 3 yrs.

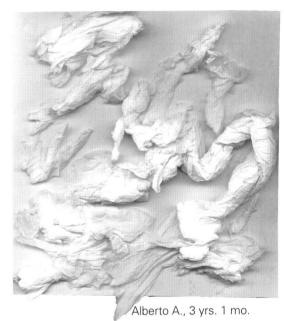

Alberto A., 3 yrs. 1 mo.

Marika, 3 yrs. 3 mos.

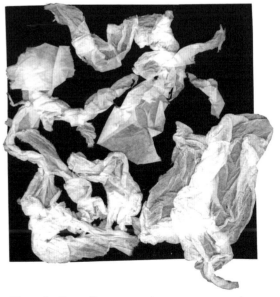

Riccardo, 3 yrs. 9 mos.

302556

compositional multiples

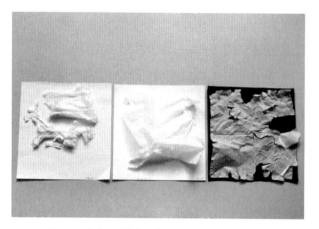 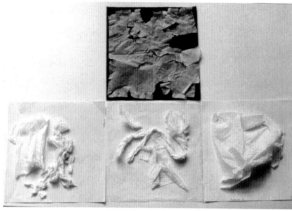 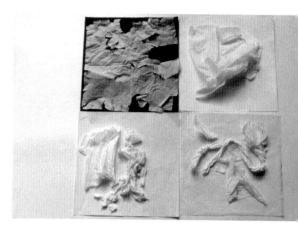

Some of the children's compositions and variations

Nina A., 3 yrs. 3 mos.
Cristian, 3 yrs. 7 mos.
John, 3 yrs. 8 mos.

The children separated, re-joined, found new perceptual arrangements, new material balances, and in the end made a choice. Modifying and varying means changing points of view, without one necessarily excluding the other.
Using a digital camera, we kept a memory of some of the compositions that the children considered to be the most interesting.

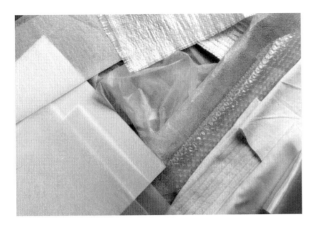

Through the game of "touch and guess" and a "tactile carpet," the children explored different material and chromatic gradations of white:

tulle - *scratchy white*, tissue paper - *music white*, terrycloth - *tickly white*, plastic - *smooth white*.

material variations of white

Numerous different materials with many gradations of white became gray, got lighter, got whiter, were illuminated, or got darker depending on the light to which they were exposed, and were transformed into a palette laid out on a table.
The children added tactility and sonority to their explorations as instruments of investigation and discovery. White materials that made sounds, gradated, smelled, scratched, and squeaked under your feet and in your hands. These were opportunities to awaken and exercise your perception: *they are soft, hard, fluffy... some of them make noise.*
The children's hands used the rituals of "listening": smoothing, scratching, "flipping over" onto their backs, poising lightly on fingertips; delicately slow, quickly jumping, making continuous circles, cautious or more hurriedly, timid or courageous, they encountered the white materials.

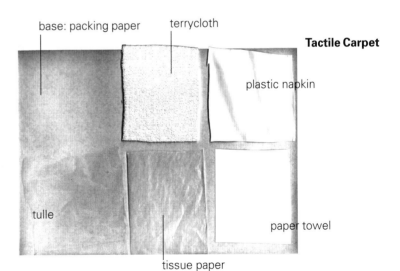

base: packing paper   terrycloth

Tactile Carpet

plastic napkin

tulle

paper towel

tissue paper

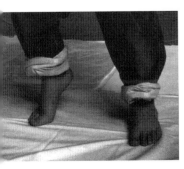

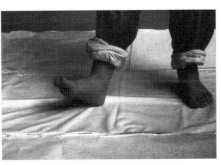

33

compositional strategies

The children were offered a sampling of white fabric, paper, and plastic.

Their curious hands rummaged around, selected, combined, and composed the materials.

The combinations were made by

similarity: *This one* (paper towel) *is this one's* (rough cotton fabric) *friend, because they're the same smoothness.*

contrast: *This one* (satin) *is cold and this one* (wool) *is warm.*

lightness: lining fabric, corn paper, slick paper, tissue paper

sheen and polish: lining fabric and satin

softness: wool, soft cotton, packing paper

grain: wool, paper towel

texture: plastic and wool with particular textures

chromatic assonance: similar whites.

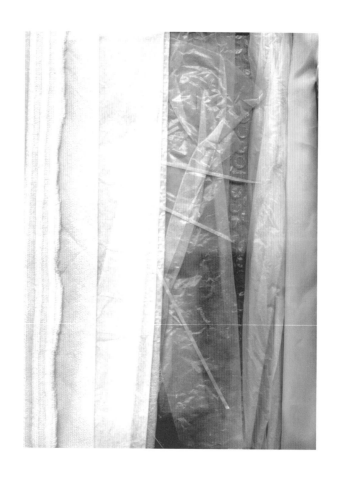

material compositions

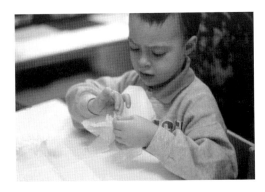

I don't know how to make these creatures.

Valerio, 3 yrs. 5 mos.

I'm pushing ...

Rudi, 3 yrs. 7 mos.

...but it just doesn't work.

The children drew suggestions from the materials themselves. Materials that were sometimes docile, sometimes fragile, not always obedient because they wouldn't hold their shape, that wiggled in your hands.
It seemed that little rituals were being established between the children and the materials, giving rise to new compositions.

Emanuela, 3 yrs. 4 mos.

Lisa, 3 yrs. 7 mos.

Francesca, 3 yrs. 8 mos.

Daniel, 3 yrs. 10 mos.

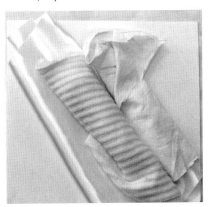

compositional multiples

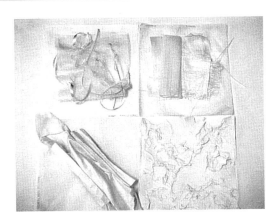

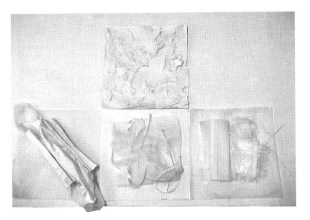

blacks
and
whites

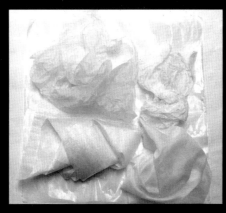
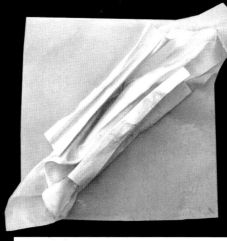
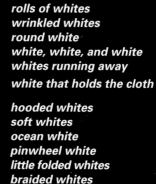

from upper left downward:

rolls of whites
wrinkled whites
round white
white, white, and white
whites running away
white that holds the cloth

hooded whites
soft whites
ocean white
pinwheel white
little folded whites
braided whites
bridge whites

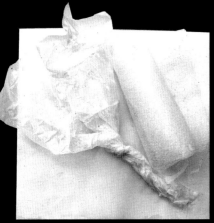
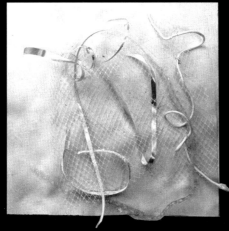

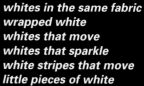

rolled whites
raised white
rolled white mountain
white holes
white with little stripes
little white squares

whites in the same fabric
wrapped white
whites that move
whites that sparkle
white stripes that move
little pieces of white

authors
children from 3 yrs.
to 3 yrs. 10 mos. old

Alberto A., Alberto L., Alessandro C.,
Alessandro M., Cecilia, Cristian,
Daniel, Emanuela, Francesca,
Francesco C., Francesco L., Giovanni,
John, Lisa, Lorenzo, Luca B., Luca F.,
Maicol, Marcello, Marika, Nina,
Noemi, Riccardo, Rudi, Valerio

the large composition

The large final composition gave the children a sense of the dimension of the work they had carried out. Each child could see himself or herself in a portion. This means recognizing yourself and distinguishing yourself in characteristics, gestures, forms, thoughts, and at the same time feeling part of a working community, able to create intelligence and beauty. The title chosen by the children at the end was "**White White White**."

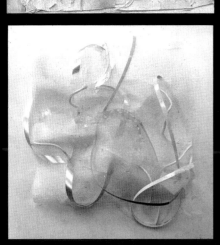

Bruno Munari Preschool
2001-2002 school year

Project coordinators
Barbara Quinti
Claudia Giudici

Elena Corte

Texts
Barbara Quinti

Photographs
Barbara Quinti
Mirella Ruozzi

Authors
five- and six-year-old children

View of work from the Munari preschool

tactile and visual
perceptions

Tactile and visual perceptions

Looking at the environment around you with new eyes to discover "lots of white material" can be a pretext for going beyond the "skin" of things.

If we then propose to the children that they create a "map of the whites in the school," we will discover how many personal and group "collections" are possible.

In this spirit, lying somewhere between play and scientific-aesthetic investigation, the children sought out and encountered the materials, and "listened" to them through visual, tactile, olfactory and auditory explorations. They organized them according to personal and original criteria, sometimes very distant from those of the adults.

In bringing materials together, the children experimented with subtle relationships by overlapping, fitting together, tying; strategies discovered and invented in getting to know the qualities and characteristics of each material in the encounter with their hands – competent and imaginative hands that appropriated the material in this way and reinvented it with unusual combinations.

Through this search for forms that were both out of the ordinary and attractive, we began to glimpse a "compositional research" on the part of the children that moved deftly from small to large scale, from very personal microcompositions to large group compositions.

The compositions were rich and precious in the choice of materials, but also in the children's gestures, which showed such variety and originality that they seemed to define a new expressive grammar.

Was it aesthetic research, then?

Not only. Underlying every compositional process are many reflections about space, form, measurement, and quantity, but also about balance and symmetry.

By their choices, the children showed that they have an aesthetic sensibility and a thought process that enable them to design, to construct relationships, and to draw strategies and procedures from other languages.

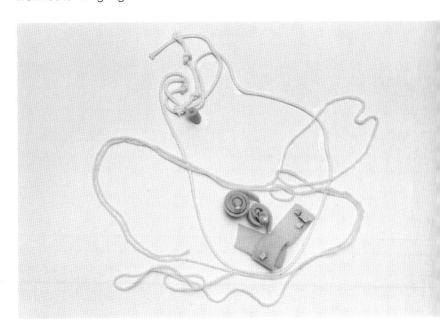

tactile and visual perceptions

What is a composition?

Compositions are when you make shapes that are beautiful, abstract; they're shapes that aren't constructions but you see them as forms. Francesca, 5 yrs. 11 mos.

They're lots of different things that are kind of special that are all spread around and they make some abstract forms. Andrea R., 6 yrs.

Putting things together means making a form, and it can also be undefined.
What abstract is, is something made of lots of materials and what comes out is a thing that you don't know what it is! The abstract starts first in your mind, then you tell it to your friends, and then it goes in the composition. If you want to understand the abstract, you can look at the drawings that very little kids make – they're always abstract! Dario, 5 yrs. 3 mos.

White was in the air, then they were born and you can see them. There are two thousand whites! Mattia, 5 yrs. 9 mos.

compositional processes

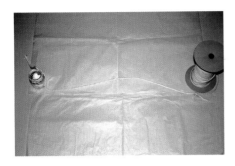

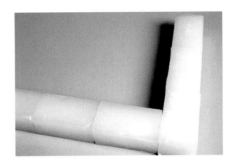

We'll take a few things, and we need some string to divide the composition…
First we need a sheet of white paper, because the gray table really isn't very pretty! Nicolò, 5 yrs. 4 mos.

I want to make a square shape. Let's start from the outside! Let's start from the corners!
Alessandro, 5 yrs. 4 mos.

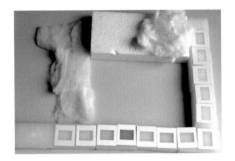

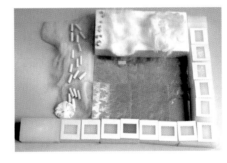

The necklace makes lots of shapes. I'll put some things inside so it'll be pretty! Camilla, 5 yrs. 11 mos.

Here's a really special thing (the fancy paper) *– let's put it in the middle!* Alessandro, 5 yrs. 4 mos.

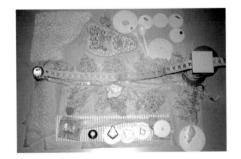

It's really beautiful. I'd call it "Angel Lightness."
Nicolò, 5 yrs. 4 mos.

In the composition you have to leave some empty space. Iman, 5 yrs. 10 mos.

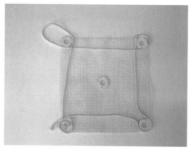

compositional processes

Why don't we put some things that hold it still, then put some things we like?
Federico M., 5 yrs. 4 mos.
String's a good idea! That way the little balls can't get out!
Simone, 5 yrs. 4 mos.

It has little dots; it's soft like an eraser!
I'm going to put these circles in the corners - perfect!
You need four because there are four corners.
Lorenzo G., 5 yrs. 4 mos.
We can wind the string around the circles! Edoardo, 5 yrs.

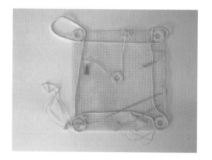

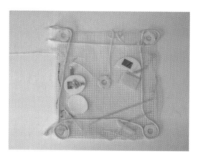

It looks like a scribble! They shouldn't be so close together.
Valentino, 5 yrs. 4 mos.

Soft plastic net...
You have to do like you're sewing! Sara, 5 yrs. 7 mos.

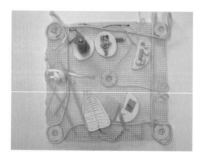

It would be better if we took all the buttons off because it's ugly. It's all spread out – I don't like it!
Federico M., 5 yrs. 4 mos.

I'm putting this leaf here so everybody can see how beautiful it is!
Lorenzo G., 5 yrs. 4 mos.

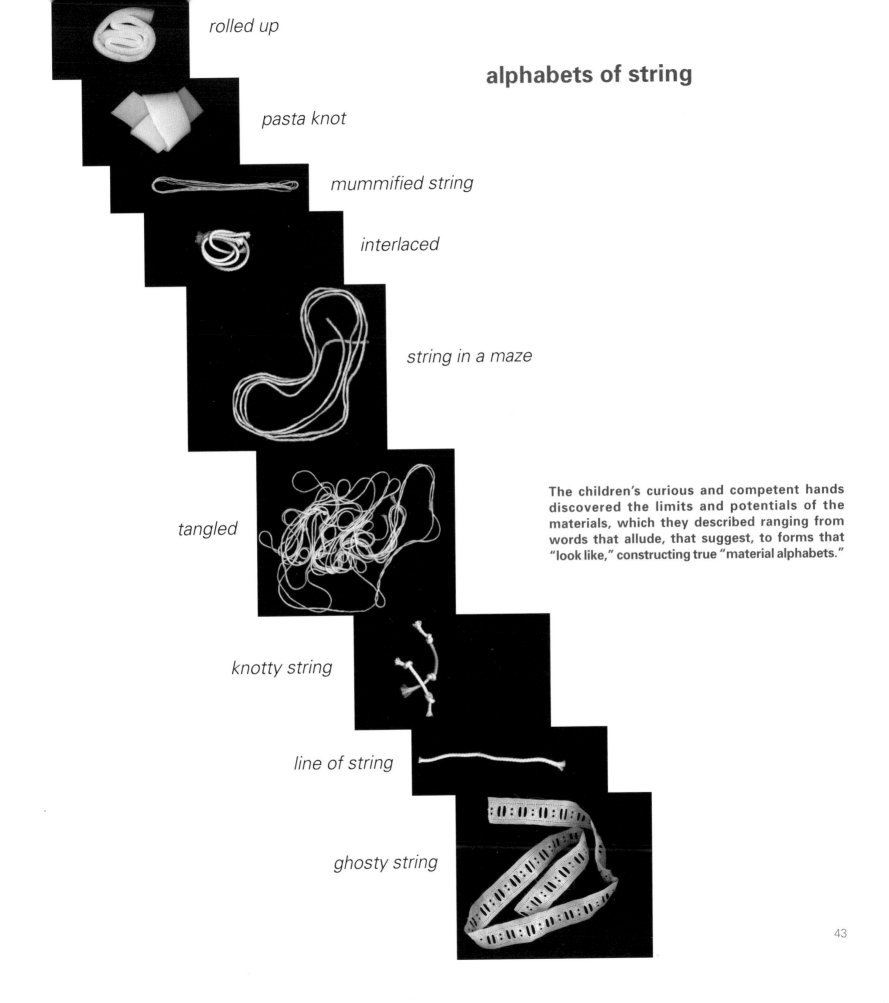

rolled up

pasta knot

mummified string

interlaced

string in a maze

alphabets of string

tangled

The children's curious and competent hands discovered the limits and potentials of the materials, which they described ranging from words that allude, that suggest, to forms that "look like," constructing true "material alphabets."

knotty string

line of string

ghosty string

You can make compositions of all the materials together that children like a lot or just one. Dario, 5 yrs. 3 mos.

Some string! Mattia, 5 yrs. 9 mos.

With the string I have to make a ghosty form! Dario, 5 yrs. 3 mos.

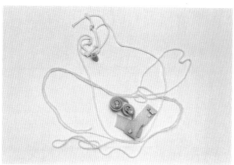

composition of string

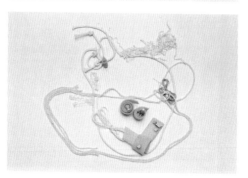

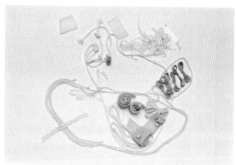

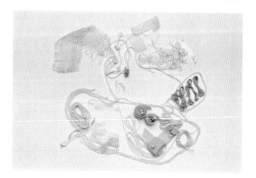

To make the composition prettier, the rubbery things have to go in the middle!
We have to mummify this string…
Dario, 5 yrs. 3 mos.

We need some glue! Mattia, 5 yrs. 9 mos.

An abstract form like this one, it's made of lots of materials melted together, so you create it abstract right from the beginning!
Dario, 5 yrs. 3 mos.

44

large composition

The beauty and originality of the children's compositions, their way of working by creating continuous relationships, internal and external, led us to consider the idea of creating a "composition of compositions" made by all the children in the class. In designing it, the children identified several common elements: the size, the decision to create mono-material or multi-material compositions, the need for the materials to be stuck together, since they had chosen to hang their compositions on the wall.

In small groups of three children each, they created nine compositions that were gradually arranged on a large piece of white cloth, chosen by the children, which helped them to evaluate the layout on a monochromatic surface similar to a wall.

The presentation of the large composition to the audience of families became a special event, a true inauguration: from the invitation to the preparation of the refreshments, all exclusively white, the children were the protagonists and authors of this event.

45

a composition is when you make something that didn't exist before Laura, 5 yrs. 6 mos.

Andrea R., 6 yrs., Camilla, 5 yrs. 11 mos., Serena, 5 yrs. 9 mos.

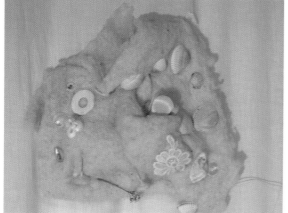

I reshaped the things and I made one whole thing Francesca, 5 yrs.

Dario, 5 yrs. 3 mos., Mattia, 5 yrs. 9 mos.,
Davide P., 5 yrs. 4 mos.

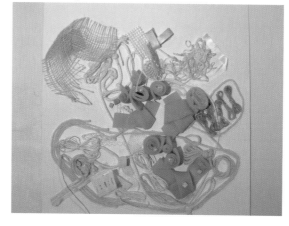

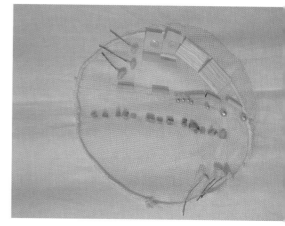

Alessandro, 5 yrs. 4 mos., Joshuah, 5 yrs. 10 mos.,
Davide L., 5 yrs. 1 mo.

Andrea V., 5 yrs. 10 mos., Valentina, 5 yrs. 1 mo.

you put the things in the places where they look good, the exact places Morgana, 5 yrs. 7 mos.

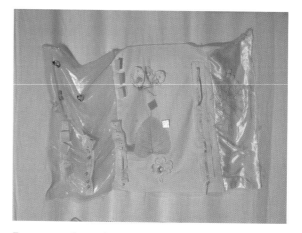

Details of the large composition

Francesca, 5 yrs. 11 mos., Edoardo, 5 yrs., Lorenzo F., 5 yrs. 6 mos.

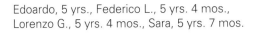
Edoardo, 5 yrs., Federico L., 5 yrs. 4 mos.,
Lorenzo G., 5 yrs. 4 mos., Sara, 5 yrs. 7 mos.

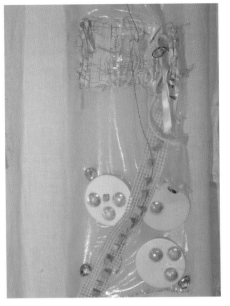

Federico M., 5 yrs. 4 mos., Simone, 5 yrs. 4 mos.,
Valentino, 5 yrs. 4 mos.

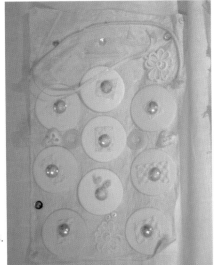

Morgana, 5 yrs. 7 mos., Nicolò, 5 yrs. 4 mos.

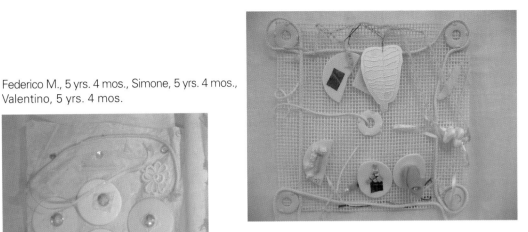

What are the children's compositional strategies?

We found analogous strategies from the infant-toddler center up through the middle school age, though with certain priorities and frequencies that differ from one age group to another.

The children composed based on different criteria:

micro-composition of correlated elements to then form a single composition

contrasts (tactile, perceptual, chromatic, dimensional)

analogies and similarities (formal, tactile, perceptual, chromatic)

symmetries

overlapping and stratification

multiplication of a single form

chance

logical relationships, evocations between form, size, quantity

sensory correlations

the sonorous quality of the materials

beauty.

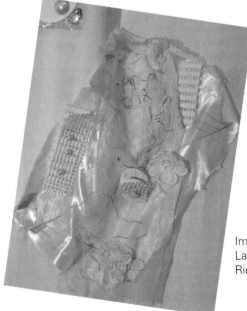

Iman, 5 yrs. 10 mos.
Laura, 5 yrs. 6 mos.
Riccardo, 5 yrs. 4 mos.

a composition seems to me like a position Nicolò, 5 yrs. 4 mos.

Iqbal Masih Preschool
2001-2002 school year

Project coordinators
Consuelo Damasi
Riccarda Bedini
Daniela Lanzi

Elisabetta De Santi
Lorena Prandi

Texts
Consuelo Damasi

Photographs
Consuelo Damasi

Authors
four- and five-year-old children

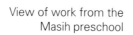

View of work from the
Masih preschool

dialogues between matter, light, and space

View of the "Plastics" section

plastics

Dialogues between matter, light, and space

While talking about plastic, the children looked around for and found it in the surrounding environment. Its presence was predominant, almost impertinent, emerging in the widest variety of forms and uses. The children touched it, tested it, and explored its various qualities with their eyes, hands, and thoughts.

It was in this moment that the idea of an installation took shape: a communicative situation in tune with contemporary life that would enable the children, who are able constructors of ideas, to create a physical impact with the surrounding environment, making it interactive, flexible, and modifiable through their explorations of materials.

So three installations were created, two inside the school – on the ceiling of the atelier and on a glass wall – and one outside, on a large tree in the school yard.

Three installations that were very different from each other but which told of original encounters, strategies, and explorations in establishing a dialogue between material and space. The idea of "big" engaged the children in their research, and they used intertwined large and small gestures to support the creation of installations that were unusual for them, establishing a relationship between material, form, and dimensions.

The installations were constructed according to different criteria, in empathy with the space-site with which they would be in dialogue, and were always balanced and delicate. The children, avid researchers of spatial designs and skillful constructors of volumes, good at calculating resistance and equilibrium, modified the environment with plays of combinations and superimpositions, creating spirals, knots, and lines that in establishing a relationship with space-environment end up transforming it.

(Only one of these three installations was shown in the exhibit.)

*The installation has
to be way up high,
because it's prettier
that way.*
Valentina, 4 yrs. 10 mos.

1

*If we turn off the light...
If there isn't any light,
our composition disappears.*
Gioia, 4 yrs. 10 mos.
*So how are we going to
keep it?*

2

dialogue between matter, light, and space

*We have to get some
plastic things that
are the same as
our composition.*
Sofia, 4 yrs. 6 mos.

3

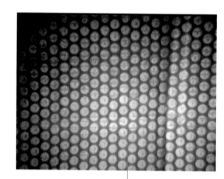

4

*We decided that even when you turn off
the projector, the composition stays there
just the same.* Valentina, 4 yrs. 10 mos.

*We need some lids
to make the bubbles
on the plastic.*
Deborah, 4 yrs. 10 mos.

5

*We need some plastic film?
to stick on the squares
of colored light.*
Miriam, 4 yrs. 7 mos.

6

From the projection to the
concrete, the girls constructed
their composition by means of
a network of tactile and visual
relationships and analogies.

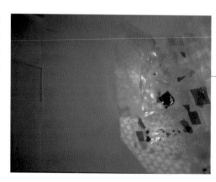

"In-stalla-stazione"
Final installation

7

plastics

in-stalla-stazione

The installation has to go way up high, because it's prettier that way…

1. **The encounters with the material were explored in more depth by a group of girls using an overhead projector. The plastic was thus investigated using light and was projected upward, onto the ceiling, a dimension not often explored by the children but which captures their spatial challenges.**

2/3. The composition of plastics arranged on the overhead projector was projected onto the ceiling, offering the girls virtual suggestions about the material.
Perceiving its impalpable and immaterial nature, the girls felt the need to "save" the projection, to make it concrete.
If there isn't any light, our composition disappears.
Gioia, 4 yrs. 10 mos.
We decided that even when you turn off the projector, the composition stays there just the same.
Valentina, 4 yrs. 10 mos.
Their intention was to return to the physical nature of the material; it seemed as if "material beckoned material," and the suggestive play of the projection demanded that its physical body be found.

4. **With the projection lowered to their height, the girls began to translate the projected forms into material forms, making use of formal and tactile analogies.**
In this passage from projection to material, they sometimes used plastics identical to those used on the overhead projector.
We have to get some plastic things that are the same as our composition.
Sofia, 4 yrs. 6 mos.

5/6. Above all, they searched for formal analogies, choosing plastics with shapes and sizes analogous to those projected.
We need some lids to make the bubbles on the plastic.
Deborah, 4 yrs. 10 mos.
We need some plastic film to stick on the squares of colored light. Miriam, 4 yrs. 7 mos.

7. The result was an installation, "In-stalla-stazione" as the girls called it [translator's note: a play on words, resulting in "in-stable-station"], that returned to its place of origin, the ceiling, taking shape in a continuous bouncing back and forth, nurtured by the luminous projection and its material concreteness.
In a sort of hybridization game, the identity of the installation fluctuated between material and immaterial.

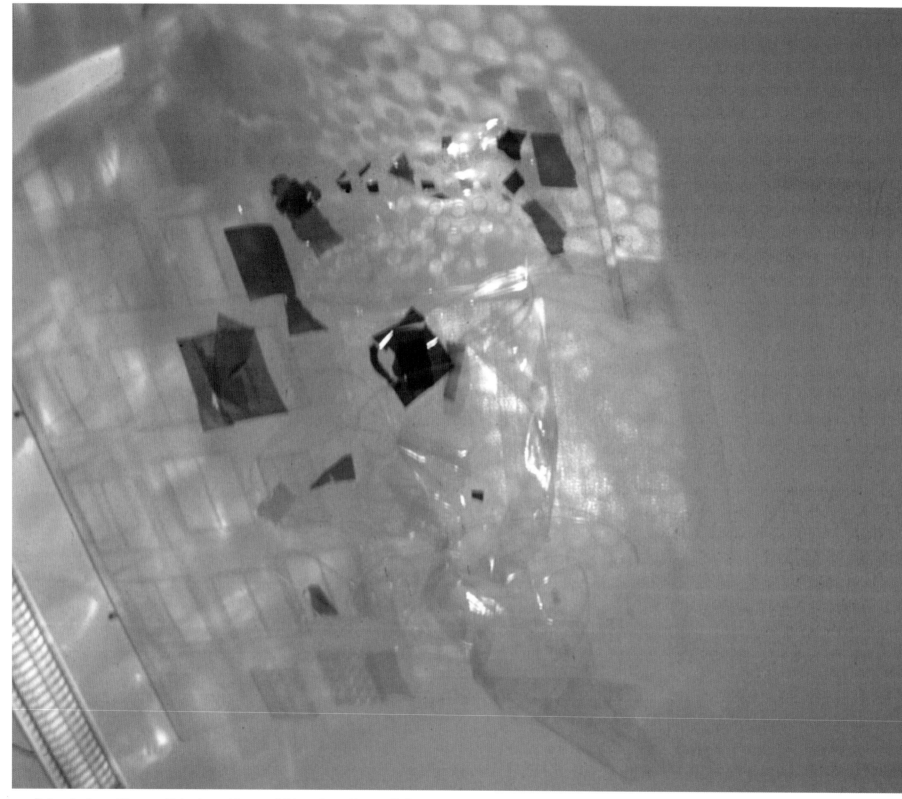

Deborah, 4 yrs. 10 mos., Gioia, 4 yrs. 10 mos., Miriam, 4 yrs. 7 mos., Sofia, 4 yrs. 6 mos., Valentina, 4 yrs. 10 mos.

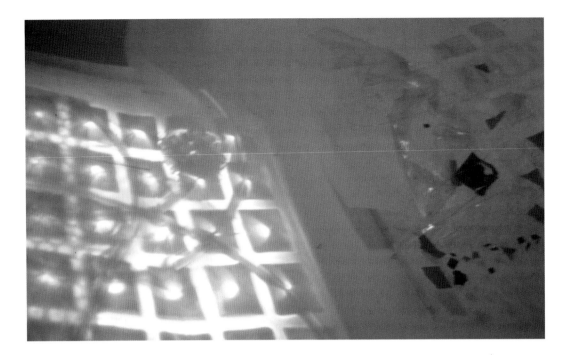

Final installation

Giovanni Fiastri Preschool (Sant'Ilario)
2001-2002 school year

Project coordinators
Filippo Chieli
Elena Maccaferri
Fausta Benassi
Maria De Biase
Lorella Trancossi

Texts
Lorella Trancossi
Filippo Chieli

Photographs
Fausta Benassi
Elena Maccaferri
Filippo Chieli

Authors
five- and six-year-old children

View of the
"Plastics" section

less than slightly
transparent

View of work from the Fiastri preschool

plastics

Less than slightly transparent

In their initial discovery of the material, the children's approach to experimentation could be defined as "global," with constant attention to all the "languages" of the material: how it can be used, its musicality, and its interaction with light, water, and air, and using their bodies and their own sensitivities.

The materials chosen by the children are very contemporary, materials that are very close to their experience: plastics with various degrees of transparency.

In approaching the material, one of the initial difficulties, perhaps the most important one, was grasping the concept of the material as matter. The children primarily saw the object, its function, color, and history, and less the material of which the object was made. In the initial conversation with the children, when we asked them: What is material? What materials are the things you see made of?, they did not discriminate between the form, the material, and the use of an object, but continuously redefined the boundaries between these concepts.

We accompanied the children in this very complex definition, supporting an informal approach for their research and trying to open their perspective to definitions that were not simplistic or rigid. We accepted their metaphors as genuine cognitive tools, capable of generating new knowledge.

The metaphors used by the children have all the characteristics identified over the centuries by the great thinkers:

Aristotle, "Metaphor is a sign of genius."

Max Black, "A metaphorical assertion can sometimes generate new knowledge and discoveries, changing the relationships between the designated objects."

Richard Boyd, "It is a sort of catachresis. They are used to introduce a theoretical terminology where such terminology did not previously exist."

Hermann Hesse, "Every theory is a metaphorical redefinition of the world."

Analyzing the transparent materials collected, the children constructed "categories of things" using metaphor, and thus created their own sample collection using a "catachresis" to introduce a synthetic theoretical terminology where their own was insufficient by itself:

mirror transparent

cloudy transparent

netted transparent

transpa

less than slightly transparent

rigid-scratchy transparent

blindtransparent

not transparent at all.

The power of discovering a concept, which is a mental category, orients the eye and the sensibility; it is at once knowledge of an object and of one's own potentials, and opens up the experimentation to different and deeper possibilities of investigation.

But discovering a concept is possible only through a multifaceted process, a process that offers new ways of looking. So we used the overhead projector, the light table, and a projector that enlarges tiny details of the materials, but also simply a window on a particularly bright day.

The discovery of the transparent occurred precisely when the children realized that there are many kinds of transparent.

The relationship with the transparent material enabled by the use of different instruments, creating the possibility to enter into it, shifted the children's attention and refined their sensibilities. With the excitement that comes from the challenge of learning, they transferred their acquired investigative ability to the different possibilities of the "transparent."

Sample collection of transparent materials

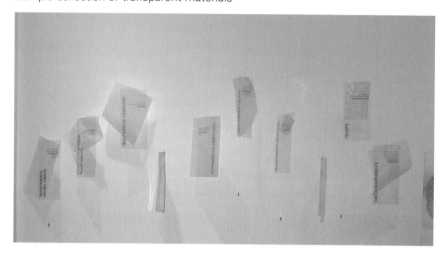

less than slightly transparent

Michele, 5 yrs. 5 mos.

less than slightly transparent...

transpa

scratchy transparent

cloudy transparent

netted transparent

wrinkly transparent

not transparent at all

veiled transparent

Alice, 5 yrs. 10 mos.

Eliz, 5 yrs. 1 mo.

Lucia, 5 yrs. 1 mo.

Vanessa, 5 yrs.

the composition makes beauty; it makes you happy when you're the one who did it Camilla, 5 yrs. 4 mos.

sculptures in water

... every time it moves, it's always different Alessandra, 5 yrs. 6 mos.

composition... maybe it's the position of a construction Luca, 5 yrs. 9 mos.

The children identified water as a transparent material right from the first conversations.
Thanks to their previous explorations, they developed an expressive concept of particular aesthetic value: one material "beckons" another material. Each composition was created using transparent materials on supports that were in turn transparent, allowing the "transparent" to express its potentials to the maximum.
The children were able to observe the transparent composition in water in all its variations in relation to light, the position of the container, and the viewing point.

View of work from the Fiastri preschool

Alice, 5 yrs. 10 mos.

Erica, 5 yrs. 6 mos.

Mattia, 5 yrs. 2 mos.

Transparent sculptures

plastics

*The computer listens to us
with the microphone; when there's
a sound it shows those
funny symbols.*

Alessandra, 5 yrs. 6 mos.

the skeleton of the sound
Camilla, 5 yrs. 4 mos.

Together with the children, and with the help of digital technology, we tried to record and display the sounds of the transparent materials. The field of action thus shifted to the sound-image relationship.

SUONO TROMBONE ↔ BRIVIDONE

SOFFIO BOTTIGLIA

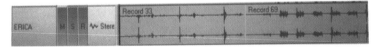

SUONO VIA E VA

Sounds displayed

*We can see our sound...
those pictures look like the sounds,
that's why the computer uses them like that.*

Mattia, 5 yrs. 2 mos.

The materials used and the composition engendered discoveries, wonder, and the need for new paths of research each time we changed the observational context.
Listening to the sound produced by a composition of little transparent tubes and strips of different materials arranged on a tree outside and moved by the wind, the children discovered new sonorities. But a tube can also be played with your breath, and a strip of plastic, made to oscillate, can be "listened to" in all its sonorous variations.

We asked ourselves and the children how we could "see" these sounds.
Using a computer with a specific program, we were able to record and display the sound bands.
The aim was to try to give a form to sound, which, by definition, is impalpable and formless.
Digital technologies thus came into play, providing new opportunities of composition between sound and graphics.

Ernesto Balducci Preschool

2001-2002 school year

Project coordinators
Mirca Neroni
Antonio Tinti
Daniela Chioffi
Daniela Lanzi
Mirella Ruozzi

Texts
Mirca Neroni
Antonio Tinti
Daniela Chioffi

Photographs
Mirca Neroni

Authors
four- and five-year-old children

General view of the "Plastics" section

brightness room

View of work from the Balducci preschool

plastics

Brightness room

Among children's expressive potentials, the language of the body is one of the most immediate and direct. It allows a total immersion, an osmotic and multi-perceptual knowledge of the world nurtured by an extremely rich grammar of gestures that generates sensations, questions, intuitions, and metaphors.

It is a way of sensing that is modulated through the possibilities of the body in movement: the delicacy and the force of gestures, the rhythm of pauses and accelerations, listening at "skin level," the alchemy of reflections, moods, and smells.

The language of the body is "improvisational," and eventually becomes ingrained, a language in which we can recognize precise individual traits. "Writings" made with the body, choreographies that make use of solos as well as a choral dimension. Choreographies constantly in relationship: with yourself, with a space, with others, with a smell, a sound, a look. Our aim was to offer the children a possible space, a space where transparency would become environment and the expressiveness of the body could encounter the expressiveness of the material. Through movement, the children explored this dimension with their whole bodies: they immersed themselves in the plastic material, bringing out its lightness and apparent immateriality, in a fluctuating and continuing transformation, like a sort of perceptual kaleidoscope. We offered the children the possibility to re-design the space by starting with a model, an experience that would take a long time to recount here.

The design potentials of the model provided an opportunity to support and give shape to the children's imaginative projections, to their "rewritings" and their desires.

I'd call it micro-project, because it's little and it's a project.

It's like a fake example.

But it can become a real room if you look at the model carefully.

Our first approach with the material, colorless transparent plastic, involved the transformation of a space in the school. We wanted to offer the children a multi-perceptual kaleidoscope that would contain different variations of the same material.

transformed space

In the hands of the children, transparency, a characteristic quality of certain plastics, was scrutinized and explored, investigated and interpreted, in the dual, boundary-crossing identity of the immaterial material. The children's bodies in movement formed a relationship with the material itself and transformed it into a whirlwind of gestures and actions... *We put the power of the world in it...* **eventually reducing the boundary zones...** *I danced with it stuck to my body...* **with an awareness that became greater and greater...** *I breathed into the plastic and then I moved with a breath... I felt like I was transparent, too.*
Body and material pursued each other, encountered and confronted each other, concealed and revealed each other, contracted and exploded, in a dance in which the children, it seemed to us, perceived an expansion of the dimensions of their own bodies, a projection that went beyond the physical nature of the gestures... *I felt like I was up there on the ceiling.*

We tried to support the children's explorations and experimentation by offering them the possibility to modify the perceptual qualities of the space using variations of light, sound, and drops of water.

brightness room

the material transforms the space

variations

The material space offered to the children was conceived as a soft, fluid stage set, open to the continuous transformations and rewritings made by the children (rewritings that ranged from adding materials to breaking them up, but also rewritings supported by narrations, suggestions, and evocations). We tried to support the children's explorations and experimentation by offering them an opportunity to modify the perceptual qualities of the space using variations of light, water, and sound. The multiple light sources and the introduction of drops of water, vaporized in the air and projected, gave the children an image of the space and an encounter with the materials that were different each time. The children investigated the sonorous potentials of the material with attention and curiosity, leading to the creation of unusual orchestrations, "noise-isms," murmurs and whispers of material with a strong evocative force.

plastics

it becomes a whole big whiteness, a whole big brightness

Filomena, 4 yrs. 7 mos.

we put the power of the world in it...

Valerio, 4 yrs. 6 mos.

we felt like we were transformed into transparents

Vanessa, 4 yrs. 5 mos.

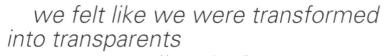

plastics

In continuity with the experimentation of a "material" place, the proposal was made to the children to design a new space.

micro-room
studies for the design of a space

We called it whiteness; it's the dancing room that we redid.

Vanessa, 4 yrs. 6 mos.

Why don't we go in with our whole selves?

It seems real to me.

Isabella, 4 yrs. 6 mos.

The creation of the room on a small scale highlighted the extreme ease with which the children grasped the translation between the two dimensions, the correspondences and analogies, to the point where the boundary between the model and the real room became hazy, got lost... and the experience they had had together re-emerged forcefully: *It's the dance that we reconstructed... Why don't we go in with our whole selves?... It seems real to me... Too bad it's so little...*

After the transparency room, the children created a "room of colors." Starting with the floor, they imagined a macro-projection and formulated hypotheses of interaction and movement in the space with their own bodies... *I thought about a floor you can jump over, so you turn around and you can run around the whole room... It looks like a maze...* The materials chosen for this purpose were transparent colored plastic bottles cut into irregular shapes that evoked images: *It looks like a maze, a trap you can't get out of; a sort of spring maze, that's it! That seems to be open but then it closes with a snap.*

The dialogue with a material that flees and withdraws drew the children into the game, engaged them in a series of tests and trials with the intent to dominate it, to bend it to their way of thinking. They came up against its force and, in the end, accepted the compromise to modify it only in part. There was a growing desire to return to the real dimension, to translate their project into a space they could inhabit and experience with their own bodies. Constructing the model, however, did not diminish this desire; rather, it heightened the children's expectations and eagerness for possible future developments.

Let's start on the ground... with the floor.
Stefano, 4 yrs. 9 mos.

First you have to look at it carefully, then you cut it the same and if it's okay, good. Then you glue the right shape, but first you cut it. Daniel, 4 yrs. 5 mos.

The floor was one of the elements that most attracted the children's attention and it became the one from which they began to design and construct the space.

To me, it's a floor that makes me think of a maze.
Stefano, 4 yrs. 9 mos.

But can't we do the walls now? Sami, 4 yrs. 3 mos.

We can make some colors that aren't there, but we have to be a little bit careful – it's hard to do!

We can put the sand wherever, just around, or in the middle... or around the middle. Isabella, 4 yrs. 11 mos.

I'd call it micro-project, because it's little and it's a project. Sami, 4 yrs. 3 mos.

We could make a room of colors, but made exactly the same as this little one. Stefano, 4 yrs. 9 mos.

It's like a fake example. Isabella, 4 yrs. 11 mos.

But it can become real if you look at the micro-project carefully. Martina B., 4 yrs. 10 mos.

Model for the "room of colors", Stefano, 4 yrs. 9 mos., Daniel, 4 yrs. 5 mos., Isabella, 4 yrs. 11 mos., Sami, 4 yrs. 3 mos.

View of work from the Balducci preschool

I breathed inside the plastics
and then I moved with one breath
Vanessa, 4 yrs. 5 mos.

View of work from the Choreia preschool

Choreia Preschool
2001-2002 school year

Project coordinators
Barbara Pini
Francesca Bianchi
Paola Cavazzoni

Texts
Barbara Pini
Francesca Bianchi

Photographs
Barbara Pini

Authors
five- and six-year-old children

light on a tightrope

Partial view

plastics

Light on a tightrope

Light is inside the body of things.
Inside people, too...
Here it's inside the plastic.

Perhaps not yet completely conscious of the experience we were about to have with the children, and possibly sharing their curiosity for this reason, one morning in the atelier we took a closer look at the transparent plastic that emerged and covered every surface and the light that suggested a multitude of explorations.

The natural light that filtered through the glass walls of the atelier moved over the plastic like a tightrope walker, playing on it and making it more seductive.

The children's eyes searched, found, traveled from a plastic sheet hanging down to a tube rising up, from the tube to a "dancing" thread, along the various nuances of the material, moving along and pausing on all the transparent plastic objects in the space. It was only through the sensitive gaze of eyes, brain, and heart that light and plastic melded together indivisibly, becoming a "single" material.

The richness of this new material was conveyed to us through the children's metaphoric and poetic language, replete with their experiences and mental images:

Light in rays
Alive light
Uproar of light.

The light passed by and through, carrying along something of the material it encountered and leaving something of itself inside the material.

In the children's minds, the light in the material not only exalted its identity but remained trapped or found refuge there, held for safekeeping.

There are lots of little tiny lights inside the plastic. It seems like there's a lot of them but really it's only one, like a string that's almost moving and makes shapes that come and go.

One of the difficulties encountered when working with children is finding ways to enable them to make their intuitions visible, to create contexts where their thoughts can continue to evolve.

plastics

fresco of light...

How children can arrive at tasting, relating to, and investigating; coming to an important encounter with the identity of the material.

... they're still all plastic,

they all have light and they all shine... because it's inside...

... light is inside the body of things...

Exploring, acting, revealing, placing layer upon layer, looking inside, removing, looking again, starting over: these were indispensable processes that the children adopted to create a new material, where light and plastic blended inseparably.

sleepmakinglight

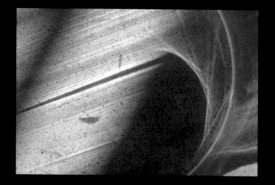

lightthatfollowsandchases

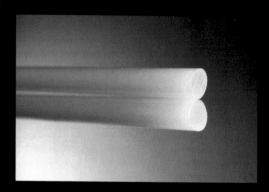

straightlight

slowlight

echooflight

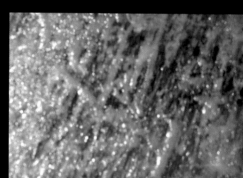

shadylight

finitelight

lightwithmorelight

proaroflight

uproaroflight

airlight

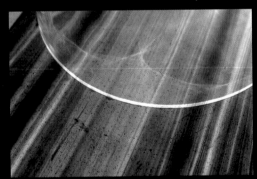

lightinrays

The words used by the children to highlight and hold onto their mental images and explorations embodied the meaning, the sense, and the metaphors they constructed in interpreting light and its variations. Image and imagination became words:

striped light

light in rays

cold light

warm light

swinging light

uproar of light

light of the air

spider web light

shady light

infinite light

light that chases

alive light

light that flies

lights mating

meeting each other

crashing into each other

dancing

Subsequently, the children interpreted and re-elaborated the material and the objects they had explored using the photographic image from a digital camera, which evoked and constructed new images, reminding us how much the virtual and the material are alive and can be experienced in a single dimension of reality.

plastics

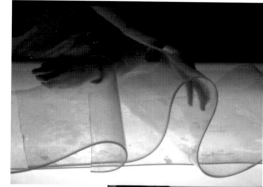

It's a memory of light,
of thoughts, it's a heavy memory,
it seems lightweight but it's
our thoughts, inside it has
the things that we said and made.
It's a memory full of light, of us.
Whoever looks at it has to be able
to see inside...
...a wave of thoughts.

Martina, 5 yrs. 9 mos.

wave of light and thoughts

A simple strip of transparent plastic could always remain an inert material, but when undulated with delicacy and intensity by Martina and Giulia, it suggested the image of a wave of light and thoughts.

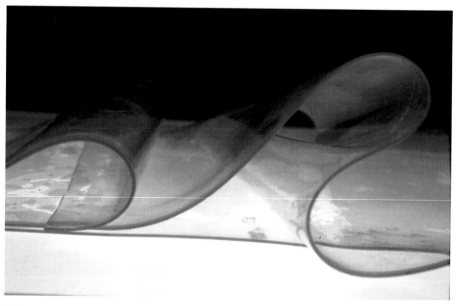

Wave of light and thoughts, Giulia, 5 yrs. 6 mos., Martina, 5 yrs. 9 mos.

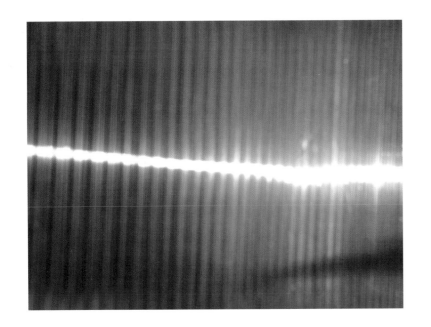

There are lots of little yellow lights inside the plastic in the form of a thread, that almost move... a thread of light that make shapes that come and go.

Laura, 5 yrs. 10 mos.

The light goes through like dancing.

Giulia, 5 yrs. 6 mos.

thread of light

My hand went all over the place; it followed the dark and the light, lighting up everything, even our bodies.

Laura, 5 yrs. 6 mos.

sewing of light

Inside the thread, here's its soul and we can see it with the light... it's really clear.

Laura, 5 yrs. 6 mos.

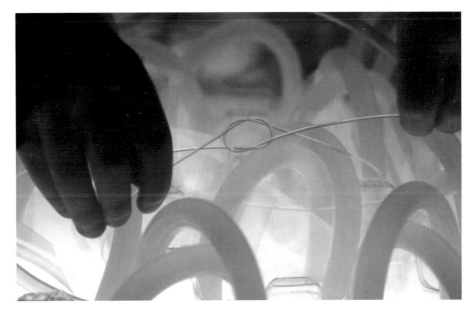

Just as when light passes through, it takes with it something of the things it encounters along the way and leaves a trace of itself, so the eyes of the children penetrated, revealed, and interpreted the things they encountered with excitement, leaving a trace of themselves.

fresco of light

If the light gets shut off, the world is shut off, too...
... The light passes through like dancing... It never stops.
In what ways could we support the children's research with light inside the material?
In what ways could we make visible the luminous substance that the children identified inside the plastic?
We decided that optical fibers could lend themselves well to our purpose, and so we handed over to the children a "thread of light" as a gift for their precious safekeeping.

I took a thin wire and I made it go around. My hand went all over the place to curl it and it followed the dark and the light.

I made a design with the wire... we used light.

Let's try putting more and more lights; there'll be my light and all of our lights... it's a creative thing all together; it's a fresco made of light.

From one thread another was born, creating imaginary planes that, in the end, constructed a luminous space. A luminous and airy installation that evoked the presence of transparent plastic in the space, making visible the luminous substance that the light left behind by crossing through it.

The children's hands intertwined with the light and with other pairs of hands to construct a transparent weaving. The threads of light crossed over each other, moved away looking for links and then returned. Gradually it became, as the children said, a "fresco made of light."

Optical fiber installation, Alessandro, 4 yrs. 11 mos., Andrea I., 5 yrs. 10 mos., Elisa, 5 yrs. 1 mo.

Gianni Rodari Preschool (Sant'Ilario)

2001-2002 school year

Project coordinators
Filippo Chieli
Elena Maccaferri
Paola Rubertelli
Sandra Garimberti
Lorella Trancossi

Texts
Lorella Trancossi
Filippo Chieli

Photographs
Filippo Chieli
Elena Maccaferri

Authors
four- and five-year-old children

View of the "Natural Materials" section

sound-making systems

Sound-making systems

The children encountered string as a material in all its aesthetic and sonorous potentials.

Variation was at the heart of our project, on different levels: variation of the types of string variation of the tension applied to the string variation of the sounds produced by the systems variation of the instruments used for creating new sounds (fingers, metal rod, bow, etc.).

Using a play on words, we could say that these "variations" resulted from "varied actions" carried out by the children, also simultaneously; that is, one type of variation did not necessarily follow the other (domino effect), but one variation replaced another in a "spiral effect," as if by sonorous analogy.

The way the children used terms for defining the materials was always extremely conceptual and not related to their common use (which in any case they are very familiar with): *soft, scratchy, tight, wide, cutting*. Words "borrowed" from a world that is not the musical one; words that have to do with the material appearance of things, in tune with the poetics of Alberto Burri. Words that must be interpreted within a context of research that is often used by the children, involving a heuristic use of analogy and the composition of categories, both concrete and formal, that are unusual for adults.

Wanting to support the children and to be able to grasp the right moment - the moment that is proximal to a leap of knowledge -, we suggested as a research strategy that the children make a graphic model before tackling the construction of the musical instrument, which was what the children wanted to do. The model drawings tended to be minimalist, synthetic, in black and white.

The graphic representation supported and guided the children's thinking, helping them to clarify their ideas; in turn, their thinking oriented the graphic representation by bringing it close to a satisfactory image, making their intentions comprehensible.

The children were perfectly aware that the object designed would then be constructed, so in creating the graphic model, they set forth the first constructive problems, simplified certain procedures, and tested the reality of their skills.

In addition, the model had a strong communicative purpose. It had to be understood by others, and required a considerable effort to step outside of one's own point of view; it became a sort of narration that put thoughts into some kind of order.

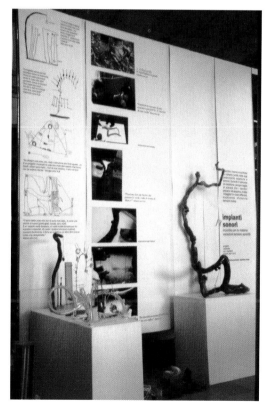

View of work from
the Rodari preschool

The grass-string *tangled up my legs.*
Valentina, 4 yrs. 6 mos.

*Maybe the sounds come from a little electric
shock and then* the sound is set off *by a string.*
Marco, 4 yrs. 8 mos.

Creating the model

sound-making systems

The children encountered string as a material in all its aesthetic
and sonorous potentials. During the project, the idea of variation,
always linked to the children's pleasure in discovering it, was
investigated in different ways, showing new and ever-changing
nuances.

*We can make some holes and pull
the string through, like Marco's shoes!*
Edoardo, 4 yrs. 6 mos.

Building the sound-making systems

I'm making a scratchy *sound;
yours was soft.*
Giada, 5 yrs.

The project originated from an outing with the children in the woods, where one of the elements that particularly stimulated their curiosity was the "grass-string," a series of little roots that tangled around their legs as they walked. Back at school, the children began to collect a large quantity of string, also bringing in a lot of material from home. Subsequently, they felt the need to create some order in their research by making a sort of list-catalogue: *dry string, shock string, elastic string, fabric string, rough string…*

The children's first instinct was to pull the strings across a space and tie them at each end with a knot; at the same time, however, they discovered the sound-making potentials of this material. They learned that if you tie a string across a space you can also pluck it, listen to its sound, and reproduce certain characteristics with your voice.

So the children decided to build some "systems" (they used this term rather than "instruments") that could produce sound and could be easily transported.
They chose two pieces of wood with particular shapes that were present in the classroom and used them to stretch the lengths of string onto.

To give more tension to the strings, they decided to make some holes in the wood like on Marco's shoes.
Giada said: *We can do it like Marco's shoes that have holes and the strings pass through them; we can make some holes on the sticks and pull the strings through them.*

Constructing the sound-making systems involved both the musical language and the visual language.
Giada: *This string isn't so much for making sounds; maybe it's just for beauty!*

Sound-making systems

Giada, 5 yrs.   Edoardo, 4 yrs. 6 mos., Marco, 4 yrs. 8 mos.

If you draw something, then when you're building it you have to make it exactly the same…
The light color ones are pretty…
They shine with the light; black in the dark doesn't show anything.

Giorgia, 4 yrs. 8 mos.

model design

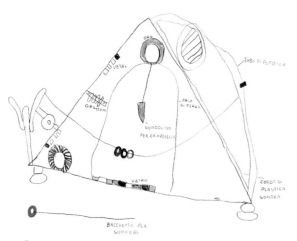

Preparatory drawings

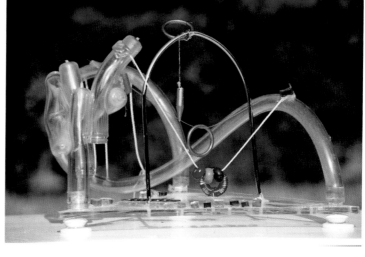

Sound-making systems

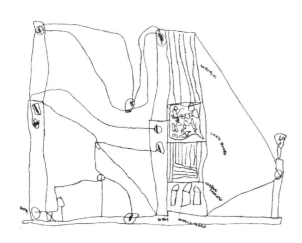

There are things that nobody's ever seen…
It's like a showcase of sounds: grated, holey, hard, soft.
It's an imaginary castle… you have to have lots of imagination to make the materials make sounds.
I used the bolts because they're musical; they're easy to play to make sounds.
If you hit the metal on another piece of metal, it makes a sound like a bell.

Marco, 4 yrs. 1 mo.

The design is for helping your
memory to remember exactly.
Before you build it, there are lots
of things you have to think about:
How do I do it?
What materials do I use?
... Then you do it, take it apart,
and ask yourself:
What was it like?
What was it like?
Eleonora, 4 yrs. 3 mos.

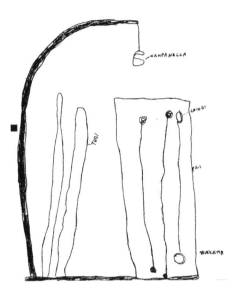

Preparatory drawings

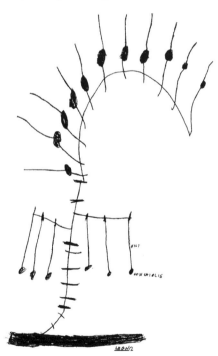

Sound-making systems

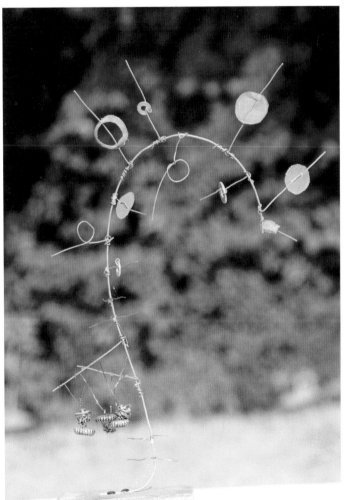

The sounds of the material,
you have to see them,
not just hear them...
It's the sound that breaks
the metal, the wood,
and the cardboard.
And it comes out.
The sound is
the material's voice.
Alex, 4 yrs. 10 mos.

81

Diana Preschool
2001-2002 school year

Project coordinators
Isabella Meninno
Laura Rubizzi
Tiziana Filippini
Vea Vecchi

Sonia Cipolla

Texts
Isabella Meninno
Laura Rubizzi

Photographs
Isabella Meninno

Authors
four- and five-year-old chidlren

View of the "Natural Materials" section

pulverized recompacted

View of work from the Diana preschool

natural materials

Pulverized Recompacted Riccardo, 4 yrs. 6 mos.

During the initial conversations on materials, the most intense discussion among the children was about things they normally find in the school yard: leaves, stones, soil, sand. So this was the direction taken in our search for materials that took place immediately afterward.

On the school grounds and in the park that surrounds the school, with a fresh eye and a sense of adventure, the children rummaged around the environment hunting for materials, observing tiny details, surfaces, colors, changes of light and shadow, experimenting with the softness of a carpet of leaves, crumbling seeds looking for material inside other material, mixing sand and dust, testing, looking, observing, enjoying. The ordinary everyday things of the park revealed it in all its extraordinariness. Autumn, harvest time. The school filled up with these materials and initially it was a bit disorienting: tables full of dirt, stones, leaves, moss, seeds, and sand, organized in containers that highlighted their characteristics. A "palette" that was both chromatic and material, but also olfactory, a big collection that the children and parents added to every day.

Here began a path of transformation, because the soil and stones were drying out, the leaves were starting to curl up and fall apart easily, so that their original consistency and color were modified naturally. Because of the children's attention to this process, the project mirrored this path of change: the classroom became a work site for transformation. The children used their hands, stones, and large sieves to break materials into pieces, crumbling them until they were pulverized, simulating and accelerating the natural path of transformation. In various containers, we kept a memory of all these steps in the reduction of the matter, these "states of matter." From leaf to leaf dust. Thus modified and transformed, the materials revealed different quantities, qualities, densities, and chromatic variations. This, too, was a powerful experience because no prediction could have offered such a confounding concreteness or such an intriguing surprise. It was another palette, but the material was the same.

Watching the children at work, it seemed that we were in a workshop for preparing colors, just like artists have always done with the pigments furnished by the earth. It is perhaps a daring parallel, but the materials actually became media for painting, and the children used this matter-material, along with other materials, for their compositions.

The compositions were made in two contexts. One experience took place again outside in the school yard, where the transformed material-color returned to its place of origin – but how? The elements of nature, sometimes in a very noticeable way, make "designs" that the children discover and comment on with curiosity. The project continued by selecting some of these natural meanderings, forms and details. The children, by mutual agreement, studied the possibilities for their own work to "continue the designs of nature" on the bark of a tree, among the branches, or on the ground, searching for "binders," materials, colors, and narrations. The other experience took place inside the school, where the children chose material combinations and composed them on supports of clay, wood, cork, leaves, and stones, some already made and some waiting to be prepared. The excitement was high, the gestures bold and courageous, quick, at times instinctive but also well thought-out. The material demanded, forced, and suggested different behaviors and actions that were well suited to the singularities of the children; it had a will of its own that encountered the will, instinct, and projective thinking of the children.

The children experimented, carried out research, sought beauty. The products were very different from each other, far from any stereotypes and close to the children's own mental images; they seemed like "musical scores" of materials. There were truly intense moments, from the beginning to the end of the project, that left deep traces in the children, perhaps because they were directly involved in the process of preparing the materials and in the creation of something that they saw as a constant invention.

A path of transformation, where the things collected in the park were modified from their original form to reveal the quantity, quality, density, and chromatic variation of the matter and become a medium for painting.

The public park of Reggio Emilia

the children's choice

Nature was the place chosen by the children to encounter the material.

The children explored the environment with their whole bodies, seeming to reawaken it.

The first transformation had begun.

Look! A bruised leaf
Carolina, 4 yrs. 7 mos.

I found the soft stuff (moss)
Riccardo, 4 yrs. 6 mos.

Stones that are warm from the sun (zones of light), *stones that are sort of dark and cool* (zones of shade)

I'm mixing the dirt and the stones, so you can't tell them apart.
Riccardo, 4 yrs. 6 mos.

Mixing was almost like inventing other material, a preview of what the children would discover later.

Their research was careful, curious, and detailed, in a realm of nature that seemed to be truly generous. Their eyes "re-designed" and interpreted the simplest things with a great deal of refinement.

Following an initial "exploratory" collection (others would be made subsequently), the material was placed in a basket and carried back to school.

back at school

The materials collected were bursting with sounds and smells. Once organized by the children in containers, the variations and the chromatic, material, and tactile characteristics of the materials were amplified. A palette of colors invaded the space. Thus ordered, the material was already beginning to weave a story about itself. The difference in humidity between outside and inside changed the colors, transparencies, and consistencies. Dirt and leaves dried out, faded, curled up, crumbled. The children intervened further to break them into pieces, crumbling and kneading together leaves and soil.

A variegated palette that was also modified by time.

mutations

Material-chromatic transformation
of a maple leaf and a hornbeam leaf

Different leaves were transformed in different ways. They changed in appearance, physiognomy, texture, and color. Some leaves became almost pulverized; others had structures that did not allow this. Breaking them up also highlighted the different color schemes on the front and back of some leaves. In nature, this transformation is a slow process; here the acceleration of the process in some way highlighted and underscored the material quality of the leaves.

spider leaves

sort of dry leaves

broken leaves

sort of hard twigs

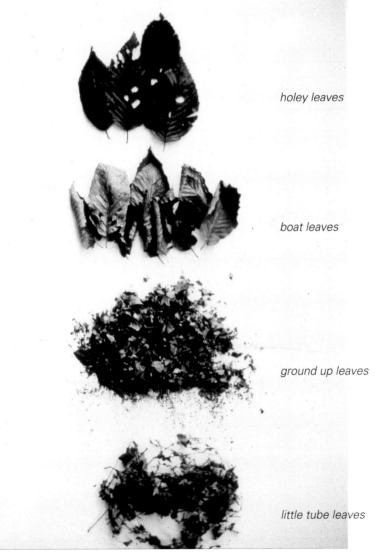

holey leaves

boat leaves

ground up leaves

little tube leaves

the work site
pulverizing, recompacting

With hands, sieves, and stones, the transformation of the materials collected continued.

Crumbling, breaking up, pulverizing.

The natural material changed from one form to another, from one consistency to another, from one density to another, from one color scheme to another, revealing variations that were almost bewildering.

The classroom was transformed into a work site.
We introduced tools such as stones and sieves. Leaves were transformed but so was clay, a material the children are very familiar with.
Crumbling, breaking up, and pulverizing until you obtained material textures that were more and more impalpable.
We invented some powders, **said the children. This work profoundly affected their research and left them with the sensation of having discovered and invented materials they did not know before.**

material-chromatic gradations of leaf and clay

snaked

brush-spread

ground up

powder

ground up with rust

spidery soft

material gradations of leaf and clay

The leaves, soil, and clay that previously had a "form" were now predominantly matter. The children gave each "state of matter" a name. These material-chromatic, olfactory, and tactile variations were reminiscent of the traditional preparation of colored pigments for painting in artisan workshops.

material palettes prepared by the children

material-chromatic, olfactory, and tactile variations
of "clay matter" and "leaf matter"

I'm photographing the universe of the tree.
Federico, 4 yrs. 8 mos.

designing with nature

The children returned to the park.

They chose small forms, spaces, and natural conformations and,

with great empathy, "continued" the designs made by nature,

also using the palette of materials prepared at school.

The matter previously removed was now returned, under a different guise, to its place of origin and used for painting and composing.

It was an osmosis between indoors and outdoors that maintained the original imprint and the bond with the natural material.

An experience that created deep bonds between the children, the park, and the natural material, which would have repercussions in other projects.

The palette of materials prepared was then used by the children to create their own compositions, which bore the mark of their different individual research.

The children composed based on criteria of overlapping, gradations, mimesis, decoration, mixtures and combinations: microcosms of marks and materials.

the compositions

At times the children followed a precise project design; at other times the will could be seen to change, as soon as it touched the matter, as if the matter spoiled the children's intentions (leaving a space of randomness and spontaneity that gratified them) and offered unexpected images. It was a dialogue: the material received, deceived, complied, resisted, was imprinted and modified quickly in the children's hands.

The compositions were combinatory trials between materials, and the children observed matter as it changed, canceled paths and modified them. Within each composition there are many compositions open to other transformations. The children explored the possibilities, the contrasts and similarities; they let themselves be seduced by the continuous and varied evocations arising from their gestures or from the matter itself.

In the final composition, we glimpsed little towers made of stones, circular chromatic paths, variations in color gradation.

Fabrizio, 3 yrs. 11 mos.

compositional process

Elia applies slip with a brush and realizes that the clay has begun to dry out:

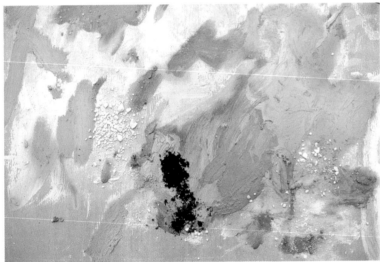

It's turning old, he comments.
The matter evokes images.

Elia, 4 yrs. 2 mos.

He etches, designs, and layers materials and powders, taking more than one day to complete his work.

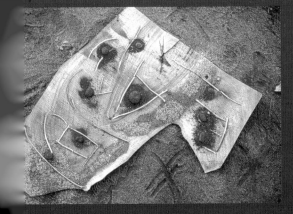

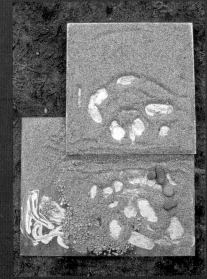

**pulverized
recomposed**

from upper left downward:

*untitled
stone and dust
lots of powders
untitled
fat line*

*sand
leaf
city work
untitled
white*

*untitled
almost black
untitled
ground up
big powder*

*untitled
little stones and sand
eighteen
untitled*

*rainbow
untitled
clay*

ring-around-the-rosy of sand
*untitled
like sand*

authors:
children from 3 yrs. 11 mos.
to 4 yrs. 10 mos.

Anssar, Anthea Ester,
Carolina, Cecilia, Claudio,
Edoardo Nicolò, Elia, Fabrizio,
Fabio, Federica, Federico,
Giorgia, Giulia C., Giulia S.,
Hamza, Ibtissam, Jeffrey,
Loris, Luana, Luca, Mattia,
Pietro, Riccardo, Salma, Sofia

Diana Preschool
2001-2002 school year

Project coordinators
Isabella Meninno
Evelina Reverberi
Tiziana Filippini
Vea Vecchi

Sandra Mercati
Paola Strozzi

Texts
Isabella Meninno
Evelina Reverberi

Photographs
Isabella Meninno

Authors
five- and six-year-old children

View of the "Natural Materials" section

formless forms

View of work from the Diana preschool

Partial view

metal and wood

Formless forms Francesco, 5 yrs. 5 mos.

The form was formed by its life Daniele, 5 yrs. 6 mos.

In general, matter appears before our eyes "changed" by industrial processing or handicraft into an object of use, becoming somehow camouflaged to our eyes and senses. Industrial processing refines, polishes, "tricks," simulates (materials that simulate other materials), and transforms the original matter.

How do the children see the material? How do they discover its characteristics?

They did so through a process of exploration that began with the objects and moved to pieces of objects that were more abstract (semi-finished products), recovering the memory of their origin.

"The form was formed by its life," said the children, who rarely separate the life and origin of a material from the form in which it appears (wood and tree). Their view is respectful and tender, but it is also a way to give meaning to the things that surround them, maintaining a connection with the circle of life that binds things together.

Then they plunged into the material, with their eyes and their touch "browsing" across the surfaces, the roughness, the imperfections, the patterns, the material qualities of sheen, color, softness, opacity, hardness, flexibility, weight, and fragility. They investigated the forms of the object-material: pointed, thin, round, jagged, linear. Material has an amazing ability to speak, to tell us about itself. It was surprising how the individual characteristics of objects "pursued" us and the way in which the children investigated them separately but immediately established relationships – using an almost instinctive approach – with the characteristics of other objects-material. These "material approaches" were arrangements-compositions that took into account a number of interesting criteria: symmetries,

balances, contrasts, and variations, which we would see again in many of their compositions.

The children, then, suggested that the investigation of the material also involved relationships, that is, composition. Reflecting on the material combinations made by the children helped us to find subsequent proposals. If, as the children suggested to us, composition acts as an intermediary for knowing and investigating, what is the basis for combining materials that are different, similar, or the same? If composing also means reconciling, constructing, and continuing, according to what rules should this reconciliation take place? We thought that one way to do this might be to search for a relationship that was even more intense than a simple combination of objects: a dialogue, a continuation, a sort of mutation of one form into another. We tried to understand which characteristics intrinsic to the object-material were the strongest for the children in this process of becoming; because one way is to consider different objects, with their own forms, separately or merely combined; another is to consider them bound by a continuum, by a development, an evolution of form and structure under other guises, in other materials.

The connection between the different materials could be found in the most intimate structure of the matter, but also in the form and color in which it appears. In combining two different forms/materials, we may find in one some characteristics of the other which, in this relationship, could be revealed. Sometimes they will be the strongest characteristics, sometimes the most evident ones, and other times the most intimate ones. It was not an easy proposal, but the children's compositions confirmed this intuition, interpreting and highlighting subtle, "superficial," or deep relationships between the materials. The compositions revealed in the material and in the objects a sort of "other" or "parallel" identity. Even the titles chosen by the children made these connections explicit. A process that sought to bind the life, form, chromatic qualities, and origin of the material, in a sort of narration.

metal and wood

formless forms
Francesco, 5 yrs. 5 mos.

the form was formed by its life
Daniele, 5 yrs. 6 mos.

Composition of bark and clay, Gloria, 4 yrs. 11 mos.

The materials are paper, metal, wood, and clay.
Miranda, 5 yrs. 4 mos.

The children suggested a sort of "catalogue of basic materials."
We focused on two of them.

Elements in metal and wood, different in shape, thickness, origin, color, and size were laid out in the atelier.

Separated from the objects to which they belonged, they became abstract elements, "singularities" to explore that immediately entered into relationships with the other materials.

pieces of metal offered to the children

material-chromatic variations of wood and metal

In a conversation about matter, the children interpreted the term "matter" with "material" and made a sort of "catalogue of basic materials." The materials were paper, metal, wood, clay. Are these the most frequent ones? The most often named? The most well-known? How do the children know the materials they listed? What images do they refer to?
These questions led us to concentrate on the variations, selecting only two of these materials. They were also large elements, elements that "decorate," have a presence, call your attention. Looking, touching, rotating, smelling, sounding, shaking, lifting, weighing; looking for variations of words to describe them became almost a necessity: *It's kind of hard, kind of soft, really hard, light, sort of hairy, rough, sharp, sort of old, indestructible, sort of shiny... it's called matte, good!* The children often began their explorations in this way, some more avidly, some in an almost scientific way, some a bit surprised, some who felt the need to "do something immediately." This is how these elements entered immediately into a relationship among themselves and with other materials.

pieces of metal offered to the children

metal and wood

the city

We're making a big city out of very strong metal. Matteo, 5 yrs. 6 mos.

The children created a large composition on the floor that they called "city." Were they guided by a symbolic image (an image that took into account the characteristics of the metal)? They worked in small groups by means of tacit agreements. Perhaps the image of the city was used to connect and keep together the many compositions within it that seemed to be dictated by little narrations, but also by the identity and the attraction of the metal material, by its structural and chromatic variations. Interesting compositional characteristics emerged, such as working with opposites: shiny/matte, smooth/rough, hard/soft, old/new, also in combining the materials: metal/plastic, metal/copper, metal/powders.

metal and powders

the city

Veronica, 4 yrs. 11 mos.
Matteo, 5 yrs. 6 mos.
Francesco, 4 yrs. 5 mos.
Miranda, 5 yrs. 4 mos.

shiny metal and matte metal

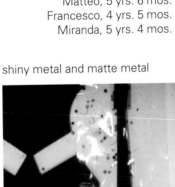

little metal, big metal, thin metal

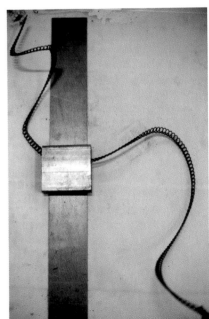

old metal, new metal, young metal

rust powder on a form of rust

compositional processes

Recovering, giving new life, approaching, transforming, continuing, adding, playing, making believe, looking for friendships, relationships, material pairings full of unusual images. The processes by which the children constructed their compositions shed light on the origin of the pieces of wood, on the meaning of the relationships between materials, forms, and colors.

1. Marta arranges two similar pieces of wood in a symmetrical, mirror-image position.

2. *That doesn't work.*

the compositions

The material environment communicated with us, the adult view became more sensitive, encountering and sustaining the immediate empathy of the children with the characteristics of the materials, the objects, the forms. A material element of metal or wood continued its life and evolved through other materials, through narration, chromatic symbology, the identity of the material, the life of the object itself.
The compositions often started with spatial organization of elements that were dissimilar or the same, that found their balance in the search for symmetry, mirror-imaging, rhythmically putting together materials that contrasted in structure, size, color, or sheen, or using all the material variations and "gradations" available. In other cases, one material seemed to search for its complement, like copper (with a contrast in material but not color), which underscored the opacity of the wood. With meticulous and sometimes almost fastidious attention, the children made their compositions. Sometimes precise, confident, sometimes clean, minimal, also rigorous, and sometimes quickly as if under dictation. Material beckoned material, color beckoned color, forms that are the same placed together, opposites and similarities attracted each other.

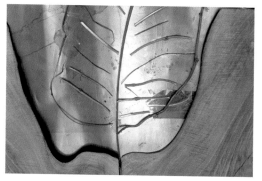

3. *It can only be like this.*
Then she takes a sheet of copper and places it as a support to the wood pieces:
This sheet of wood has some veins and this sheet of copper looks like it does.

4. On the sheet of copper, she draws a leaf with some branches:
Now the wood and the copper are friends; before that they weren't, because they didn't go together.

Incredible form, wood and copper
Marta, 5 yrs. 7 mos. and Miranda, 4 yrs. 4 mos

metal and wood

1. Francesco chooses a square piece of metal with a raised diamond texture. He takes the clay, makes some slabs and places them around the piece of metal.

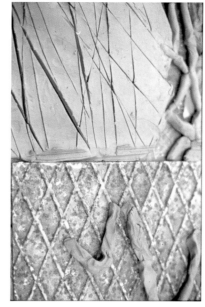

2. Using a spatula, he traces the diamond pattern and continues until he reproduces it on the clay.

3. Using other clay slabs, he takes imprints from the pattern on the metal and reproduces it a number of times.

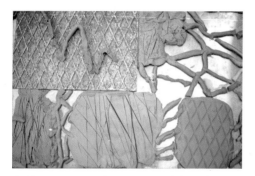

4. He arranges them around the piece of metal like islands and archipelagos, and connects them to the others using strips of clay that again recall the texture of the metal.

Formless forms,
iron and clay

Francesco, 5 yrs. 5 mos.
Manuel, 5 yrs. 5 mos.

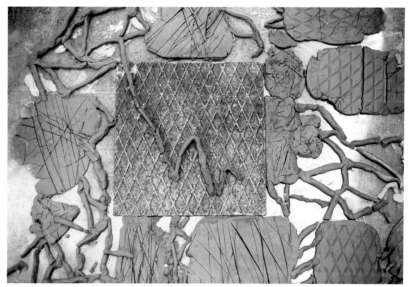

5. *They're unformed with the form of the metal.*
The metal element is the matrix from which the clay draws its pattern, reproducing it, highlighting the structure, interpreting it.
The different forms that are constructed thus have a common origin.

103

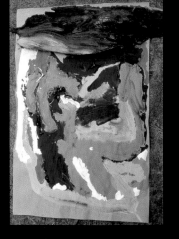
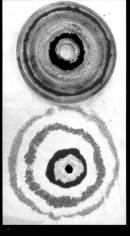

formless forms

from upper left:

incredible form
same wood, different wood
sand, salt, coarse salt, orange metal
'You have to look at the wood'
forms that are round, precious, shiny
city, bridge, parks, sand, metal dust, plastic

formless forms from the metal
yellowish material. wood level 1
dark red material. wood level 2
marks on the bark

three colors: little stones, big stones, sand wood
pure tree, jokes between wood paper clay
interlacing
powerful metal

veins of wood, sand, stones, fire red
magic white dug up earth and little stones
composition of bark and clay
friend logs
sort of the same, sort of different
shiny, old, soft metal, really hard sharp metal

authors:
children from 4 yrs. 11 mos. to 5 yrs. 9 mos. old

Alice, Andrea B., Andrea C., Andrea D., Antonietta, Bettina, Chiara, Daniel, Daniele, Davide, Edoardo, Eleonora, Elikem, Emanuele, Federico, Francesco, Giulia, Gloria, Laura, Manuel, Marta, Matteo, Miranda, Oumar, Paolo, Veronica, Vincenzo

Annunziata Bergonzi Elementary School
School Year 2001 - 2002

Project Coordinators
Maria Grazia Stefanini
Mirella Ruozzi
Lorella Prandi
Vania Zannoni

Texts
Maria Grazia Stefanini
Lorella Prandi

Photographs
Mirella Ruozzi

Authors
Seven- and nine-yearold children

General view of the
"Mix of Materials" section

in the world of forms
and materials

Exhibit of work from Bergonzi Elementary School

mix of materials

In the world of forms and materials

This project adopted a broad cultural perspective, addressing issues such as the place of modern art in elementary school. We discussed this particular topic in view of the fact that elementary schools often neglect or deliberately avoid a number of aspects that actually have a deep impact on life, knowledge, emotions, and aesthetics. These aspects continue to be considered as marginal in elementary schools because we are too busy concentrating on the specific subjects that have to be covered, which are still often considered as the only sources of culture and knowledge.

Introducing modern art in school is something that upsets the rules. Indeed, modern art means turning things upside-down, improvising, designing new projects; it means fluidity, emotion, imagination, and rationality, the freedom of the times and so on, which is the opposite of what is expected and codified. All this cannot be provided for by predefined programs in which the centrality of the children's knowledge-building processes – which require long and flexible timeframes and to allow for the possibility of constantly adjusting the initial goals – does not always or easily fit in with other priorities. According to Edgar Morin, all our teaching activities are geared toward programs, while life requires strategies and, where possible, serendipity and art.[1]

The project involving the encounter with Burri's art was significant and broad-based, allowing for the possibility of being adapted to the direction taken by the children and linked with their living contexts. It also provided yet another opportunity to observe children as they discover things, to see how they establish relationships with each other and the surrounding context, how they put forward their suggestions, discoveries, and what they learn, with their individual timeframes, methods, and strategies.

It is important that elementary schools go back to working on broad-based projects and that time be reallocated to reflecting and developing ideas that combine our different skills. These ideas should be brought together with those of the children who, with their insights and enthusiasm, know how to be active participants in the construction of their own knowledge and can be a source of knowledge for us as adults.

Schoolwork also means pursuing activities which, through art, cut across many other disciplines, and thereby attribute meaning to them and set them within a meaningful context, highlighting the connections of each discipline with the wider context. Morin states that even if we cannot always make connections between different knowledge areas, we can still contextualize topics and thereby create connections between disciplines. This means dealing with knowledge in a more comprehensive way and, at the same time, getting into the habit of being more mentally elastic.

In our elementary schools, there are neither atelieristas nor ateliers with their plentiful supply of stimulating materials. Usually, or if a school is lucky, there is a classroom equipped with paintbrushes and paints where children go and paint. The school in which this project was carried out has a multi-purpose classroom that is still in the process of being completed. This room, where children from different classes in the same grade can engage in various activities, including painting, was the space we used for the activities of this project.

Our intention was that material should be the main player from the very beginning and would instill an enthusiasm and excitement to do things. A great deal of attention was therefore devoted to selecting and presenting the materials. The children were invited to select the materials individually and to explain the reasons for their choice to their classmates. We realized that, as the children explored, they were developing strong powers of observation. The children, in fact, were using different channels of perception such as sight, touch, hearing and smell, so that after a number of sessions in which a simple initial classification of the materials was performed, the materials gradually acquired a stronger identity and richer perceptive qualities.

The fact that light was referred to on several occasions as an element of transformation, sparked off the idea of arranging an encounter between light and materials through the overhead projector. Using this tool, the children discovered and rediscovered materials and their hidden nature such as the weave of a gauze cloth, the transparence of a silver strip, and the brilliance of stones.

The light transforms things and plays tricks, commented one child.

It retains the characteristics of all the materials, creating large frescoes.

The materials acquired a new fascination and suggested new narratives.

- *Is it a copper plate covered in little holes... or... is it Paris by night?*

At this point, the work of the two classes (second and third grade) taking part in the project started to develop along different paths. The children in the second grade spent more time exploring the materials with the overhead projector, creating large images projected onto the wall and simultaneously voicing many evocations.

In the classroom, outside of the specific workshop sessions, the children were inventing stories connected with these images. Seeing the freedom and pleasure shown by the children

in their response, we thought we could suggest that they construct stories with materials as the characters, carefully ensuring that the singularity of the materials would be maintained. The stories were invented in small groups made up of three or four children. First they were told verbally and then "dramatized" through the overhead projections.

We subsequently decided together with the children to write a sort of "identity card" of the previously selected materials. The idea of this request was to sustain their relationship with the materials. From the very beginning of the experience, our hope was that the children should look at the various materials as different identities to be "listened to," to develop a way of looking at things that also contains the ability to listen to them. The children constructed the identity cards, finding a number of different adjectives to refer to the selected materials. Then, looking through different typographical characters, they found an "expressive typeface" to suit the chosen adjectives and used the computer to combine the text with the previously scanned image of the relevant material.

The children in the third grade took a different approach and developed their relationship with the material by making compositions with it. We found it interesting to observe how children dealt with composition and the perceptual and imaginative strategies they used. They worked in pairs and small groups, as they had a lot of materials to work with. To begin with, they seemed to be rushing through them, apparently attracted by the sheer quantity of the materials. In the subsequent stage, their choice became more deliberate and the selections they made were based on aesthetic and compositional pleasure. When the time came for them to present their work to their classmates, they explained their compositional criteria clearly.

Later, in groups of two or three, they looked for verbal adjectives that could express some of their compositions. With the adjectives they found, they made a verbal composition that would formally match the relevant composition of materials, providing a "visual text" that could represent their compositions through a different language. This way, they played around with shapes, colors, and meanings: an interesting exercise that nurtures linguistic, analogical, and expressive skills and, more particularly, generates the habit of making connections between things and aspects that may appear to be very distant from each other.

At this stage of their work, the visit to the Alberto Burri exhibit took place, preceded by the activities of the expressive workshops conducted alongside the exhibit. The theoretical and procedural contents of these activities bore a close affinity to the work done at school.

In their encounter with Burri's works, the children certainly showed a keen sense of awareness and attentiveness. They said, almost in surprise:

All the work we did had to do with Burri. We glued things like him and used a lot of materials. He used a lot of metal though, with all those cuts!... How did he manage to sew metal?

He used two colors a lot: whites and blacks... Black is a color, too. As a matter of fact, there are a lot of black colors.

Back at school, we looked over and discussed our compositions. The last suggestion we put to the children was that they should document the composition process of a new piece of work. Each group was made up of five children, with two children in each group appointed to take care of the documentation. One of them used the digital camera to take photographs, while the other asked questions, taped the answers, observed, and noted down the things that struck him or her as important.

Documenting processes is a fairly complex exercise, thus all we can do here is to note the procedures followed by the children. Documentation is a remarkable tool of self-education and for gaining knowledge about children. As such, is a precious tool for the teachers as well as for the children themselves. It helps to improve understanding, to attribute meaning to what is being done, and to learn how to learn. Ultimately, it generates approaches and strategies that are acquired through concrete and frequent action.

This is only the beginning, but we realize that the children have the necessary skills to continue and develop this course of action. The ability to consider the same problem from several viewpoints, together with factors such as flexibility and fluidity of thinking, teamwork, and creativity are going to be increasingly sought-after in the modern world. It seems to us that the work we did in this project steered us in this direction.

Note
1. Edgar Morin, *La tête bien faite*, Editions Du Seuil, Paris, 1999

in the world of forms and materials

The children examined and explored
the various materials in order to discover
the singularity of each.

*It's a crystal castle,
as light as fairies...*
Letizia, 7 yrs. 2 mos.

The children in the second grade
encountered a rich display of plastics
and lightweight transparent fabrics,
which had an immediate and strong
narrative impact.

The children in the third grade
found the materials piled up
on the floor, arranged in a
semi-circle of various colors
and materials.

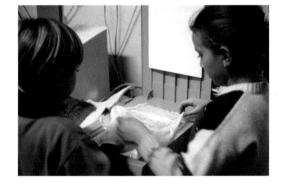

Explorations with the overhead projector

The children wrote, composed,
and invented a sort of "identity card"
of the materials using the computer
and the scanner. These tools underscored
the extent to which digital technology
can be used to buttress the expressive
aspects of the work.

*Gauze cloth is smooth and soft, it's made
of fabric and, if you look through it,
it whitens... I think this kind of writing
is very good for writing that gauze cloth
is transparent.*
Gaia, 7 yrs. 6 mos.

*- Is it a copper plate covered in little holes...
or... is it Paris by night?*
Mudi, 8 yrs. 7 mos.

TULLE

È bianco
Soffice
Bellissimo
Morbido
Sembra la stoffa del vestito della sposa
e anche la sottoveste
E' liscio come la paglia
Fa vedere tutto attraverso :
è trasparente
è il più leggero,
se lo sfreghi fa un rumore
piccolissimo.

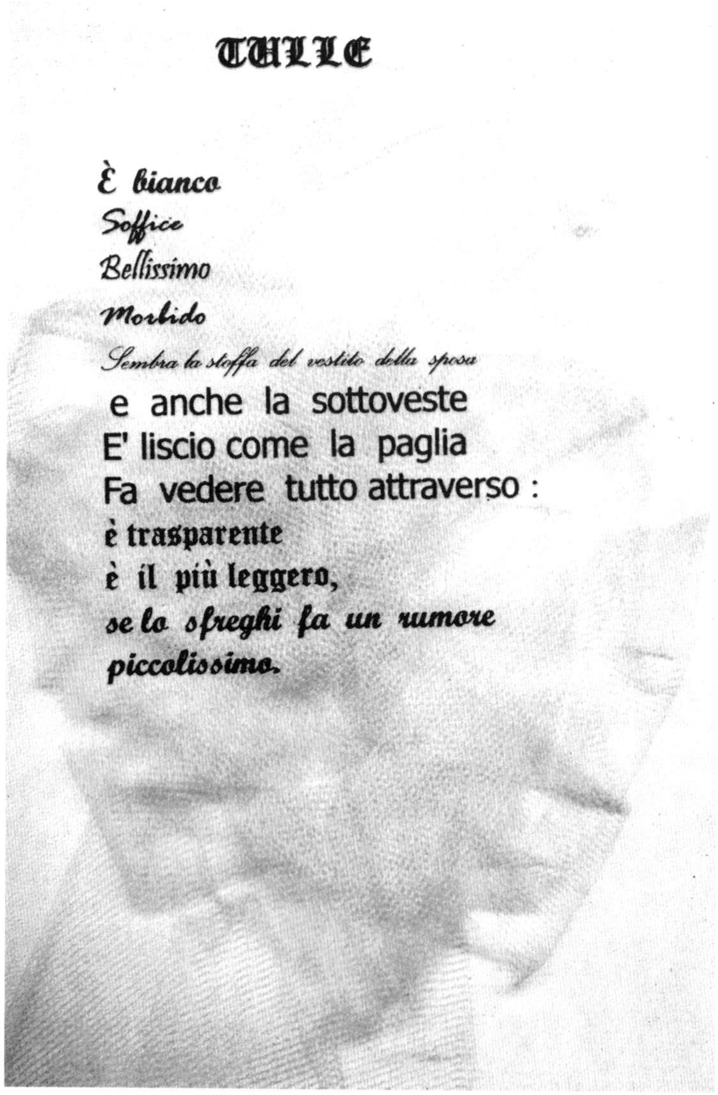

The children used the computer to construct the "identity card" of the materials, finding the right adjectives for the materials they were referring to. They also made an interesting search for an expressive typeface that would suit the selected adjectives. In order to do this, they experimented with the different typographical characters available on the computer word processing program.
Finally, they went on to construct the identity card of the selected material, matching the image of the material they had previously scanned with the relevant description.
The experience of scanning the chosen materials and reworking the images by selecting, enlarging and changing them was very interesting and engaging.

in the world of forms and materials

silver strip

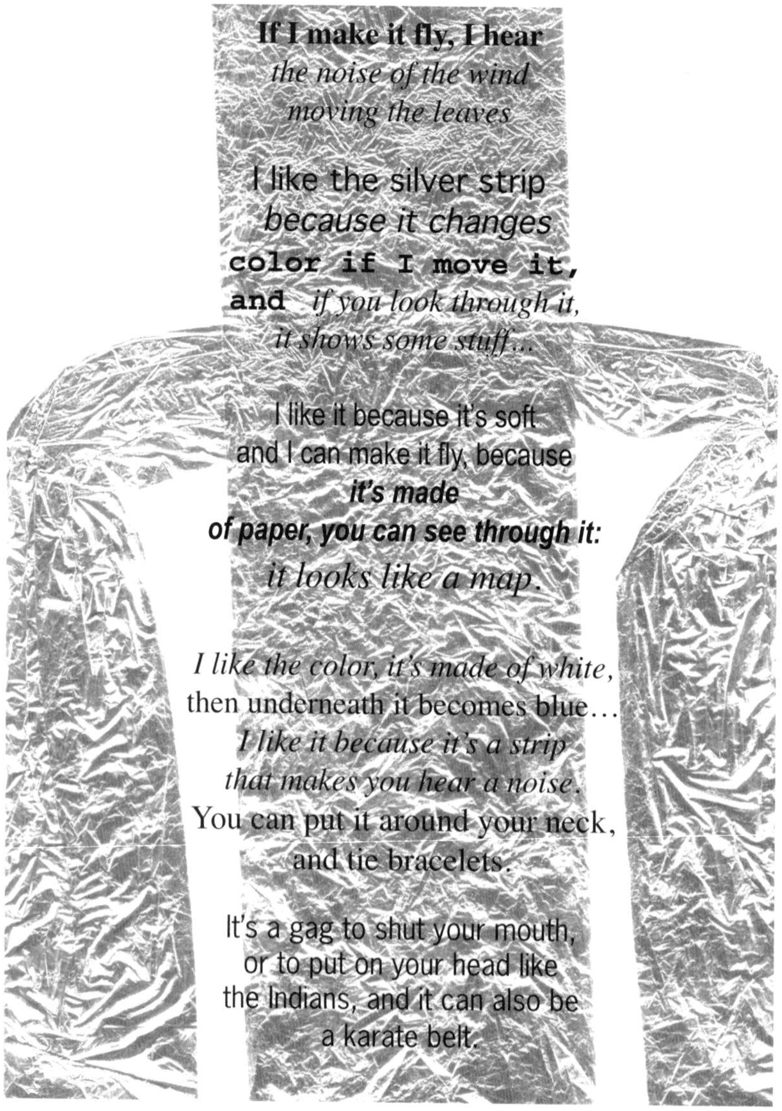

If I make it fly, I hear
the noise of the wind
moving the leaves

I like the silver strip
because it changes
color if I move it,
and if you look through it,
it shows some stuff...

I like it because it's soft
and I can make it fly, because
it's made
of paper, you can see through it:
it looks like a map.

I like the color, it's made of white,
then underneath it becomes blue...
I like it because it's a strip
that makes you hear a noise.
You can put it around your neck,
and tie bracelets.

It's a gag to shut your mouth,
or to put on your head like
the Indians, and it can also be
a karate belt.

"Identity card" of a silver strip

Narrations using the overhead projector

Once upon a time, there was a piece of hard plastic that kept stinging everyone. It was called Sting. Sting's mom, a big square piece of plastic, was hard and red, and his cousins were called Little Sponge and Little-Big Sponge. He had two more called Transparent and Little Velvet. When Sting played football with his cousins, he would puncture the ball. When he had to say 'Nice to meet you', he would sting. So, nobody wanted him a he got left out of things. He felt very lonely. But one day, his cousins said to him: "Sting, when you have to say 'nice to meet you', don't be so stiff. Relax a bit more so you can move your stings without hurting anybody. That way, everyone will want you to play with them."

Daniele, 7 yrs. 4 mos.
Letizia, 8 yrs.
Maria Beatrice, 7 yrs. 6 mos.
Marta, 7 yrs. 6 mos.

**After many exploratory activities and encounters with the materials, a number of stories started to emerge.
As they were inventing, the children were discussing things, attempting self-management and occasionally engaging in lucidly critical self-evaluation.**

I think when we're inventing stories we can't decide some things, like who should speak, for example. Someone wanted to add a piece but there wasn't enough time and then we weren't putting in the details. We lost some ideas.

The children then narrated these stories to their classmates using the overhead projector. The atmosphere this created boosted their imagination and made them change their stories slightly. During the narration, a number of recordings were made with the video camera which became the highlight of the school's Christmas show for the parents.

*We chose all the gray and black materials
and put one inside the other at random.*

Fabio, 8 yrs. 3 mos.
Laura, 8 yrs. 8 mos.
Marco, 8 yrs. 8 mos.

It's a composition of compositions!
Marco, 8 yrs. 8 mos.

*We broke off the bits of silver strip,
but we didn't know where to put them,
so we picked them up and let
them go where they wanted.
We opened the window and the air
showed them where to go...*

Rossella, 8 yrs. 3 mos.
Valentina, 8 yrs. 6 mos.
Stefano, 8 yrs. 6 mos.

*First of all, we chose two round shapes.
They were black, nice, and hard.
We liked them because of the shape: a sort of D-shape.
We took some dark colors and then wanted to put in more...
The copper sparkled against the light and
looked good with black underneath.
The strip with threads going across it,
some of them broken, gives a sense of movement,
that way they're interwoven, lifted up, broken off,
wavy, none of them straight, going up and down,
going into each other, one on top of the other.
The way the light goes over them is important.
We need to think about it to decide how to arrange things.*

Federico, 8 yrs. 9 mos.
Andrea, 8 yrs. 6 mos.
Alessandro, 8 yrs. 3 mos.

mix of materials

Marika, 8 yrs. 4 mos.
Tiziana, 8 yrs. 2 mos.

We grouped things according to color,
we really thought about the colors.
We added black to make them stand out more...
We decided that at the beginning.
We think colors always look real good in things.

The same materials used in the course of the work acquired different lives and meanings which they certainly never had before. The children experimented with various concepts such as transparence, weight, changing shapes, and sound. They examined the relationship of materials with light and the way it highlighted some of their qualities. They redeveloped expressively the meaning of some of the materials. As they were combining the materials in their composition, they had become more aware of what they were doing, making less random and more conscious choices. They were trying out combinations, superimpositions, and new transparencies while listening to each other, arguing, and reaching agreement.

Mudi, 8 yrs. 7 mos.
Salvatore, 8 yrs. 9 mos.
Anna, 8 yrs. 3 mos.

We laid the materials on top of one another,
from the large to the small one...
Then we took off and added on...
With lots of colors that looked good together.

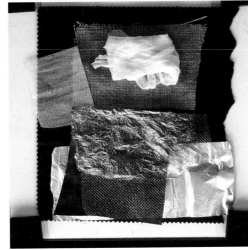

Sara, 8 yrs. 3 mos.
Simone, 8 yrs. 6 mos.
Svieta, 9 yrs. 1 mo.

We tried to combine things...
We started with black velvet
and added other objects...
... It came out just like that.
Sometimes we don't realize what we're doing.
We put in some square fabrics.
We folded the gauze to make it square!
The aluminum strip underneath is bright,
it gives out a lot of light!

children as documenters

What does it mean to children to be observing and documenting the strategies and learning processes of their peers as they go about arranging their compositions?

Documenting processes is a fairly complex exercise, thus all we can do here is note the procedures followed by the children. Nowadays, the visibility of (individual and group) processes is widely regarded as a crucial factor.
Documentation is a remarkable tool of self-education and for gaining knowledge about children. As such, is a precious tool for the teachers as well as for the children themselves. It helps to improve understanding, to attribute meaning to what is being done, and to learn how to learn. Ultimately, it generates approaches and strategies that are acquired through concrete and frequent action.

mix of materials

This piece of plastic is quite big, it's flat and it's like a base... the red cardboard is a bit smaller and colored, so we can put something on top.
Chiara, 8 yrs. 11 mos.

Why did you like this strip of metal?
Federico (documenter), 8 yrs. 8 mos.

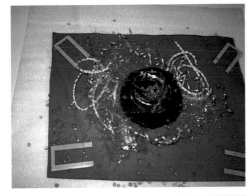

At first we didn't like it, but then we rolled it up and it became really beautiful.
Marta, 8 yrs. 2 mos.

We liked the netting because it covered everything and we put in the red woolly knobs around the edge because it was too white outside.
Svieta, 9 yrs. 1 mo.

The works of peers elicited words and adjectives, sounds and rhythms, and new mental images which the children then used to make word compositions, producing a visual text that could adequately represent the compositions of materials.

from matter to words

Federico, 8 yrs. 11 mos.

Marco, 8 yrs. 11 mos.

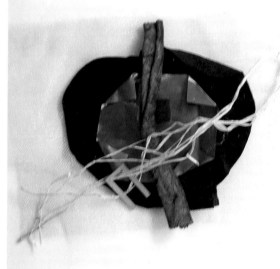

Giulia, Chiara, Edoardo

Ilenia, 9 yrs.

Anna, 8 yrs. 6 mos.

Marta, 8 yrs. 5 mos.

This is an interesting exercise which nurtures linguistic, analogical, and expressive skills and, more particularly, generates the habit of making connections between elements that may appear to be very distant from one other.

Giancarlo, Federico, Raffaella

119

Expressive workshops

Project coordinators
Ines Bertolini
Elisabetta Farioli
Vea Vecchi

Workshops conducted by
Rossana Bianchini
Sara Bompani
Giorgia Cantoni
Renza Grossi
Sabina Lugli
Roberta Pedroni

Texts
Renza Grossi

Photographs
Claudio Cigarini
Andrea Zamboni

General view of the elementary school and expressive workshops

Expressive workshops exhibit

Expressive workshops conducted alongside the Alberto Burri exhibit

The project was designed to be consistent with the experimental approach that the Civic Museums have been adopting for some years now to try and boost the cultural relevance of their relationship with local schools. A new and significant element introduced in this project compared with traditional school visits was to arrange for workshop activities to take place prior to visiting the exhibit. Our aim was to try, as far as possible, to avoid producing formal simulations of Burri's works which would have been a betrayal of his work. Our intention was primarily to offer children and teachers various opportunities to explore and approach the materials. Such opportunities were suggested by some aspects of Burri's work that also had the potential to establish a dialogue with the children.

The guided visit to the exhibit was conducted by teachers (who had had the opportunity to examine more closely the work of Alberto Burri at a number of previous meetings), in collaboration with docents available throughout the exhibit to answer any questions and clarify any points.

Those working in this field are very familiar with the problems connected with the amount of time taken by workshop activities and the large numbers of children and youth visiting the exhibit simultaneously. They are also well aware of other important issues such as the professional preparation of the staff and the organization of the work.

whites and blacks
chromatic gradations

materials

Black and white objects of various shapes, sizes, surfaces, and material qualities.

The children were presented with these materials and invited to explore and comment on them with a view to developing their perception of chromatic gradations.

procedures

The children sat in front of two "paths" of materials, one containing various chromatic gradations of whites and the other of blacks.

They examined, touched, described, and interpreted the materials through their senses, feelings, and evocations.

They then individually chose the materials they found most interesting, brought them to the table and started to make compositions with them.

Subsequently, each person's composition was used, in whole or in part, to make joint compositions. The compositions were then photographed with a digital camera and discussed by the whole class.

white can be:

transparent white
wax white
opaque white
yellowed white
pierced white
ugly white
coarse white
plasticized white
paper white
flat white
shiny white
brilliant white
custard white
dotted white
cream white
granite white
off-white

black can be:

transparent black
shiny black
funeral black
wool black
soft black
thread-like black
heavy black
pierced black
strange black
thick black
thin black
smooth black
reflecting black
pleasant-to-touch black
wrinkly black
sparkling black
net black

Projection of the scanned images of the compositions

joint compositions of colored forms

*when we joined our colored forms
together we got the feeling
of an explosion!*

materials

Paper sheets of various sizes, colors, and thickness;
packaging paper, drawing paper, tissue paper, transparent,
matte, glossy, translucent paper, and wallpaper;
smooth and wrinkly papers with different
textures and material properties.
Black pencils and different color oil pastels.
Scissors.

The oil pastels allowed the children to make color variations by
smudging, shading, and scraping the color from the sheet and
putting layers of different colors together. The soft and malleable
oil paste adapts easily to the surfaces of different materials,
becoming an integral part of the work, and altering the effect of
the color itself as it creates a dialogue with the "host" material
underneath it.

procedures

The children were divided into two groups working at two tables
covered with different kinds of paper. They were then asked to
"listen" to the material quality of the paper with their hands, to
examine them close up and choose the ones they found most
interesting.

It was suggested to them that they make one or more non-
figurative forms colored with oil pastels that would then be cut
out. Cutting out allows the form to be redesigned.

At each table, the individually produced forms were then placed
on a large white or black sheet, to make up a single large joint
composition. The two compositions were then photographed
with a digital camera and discussed by the whole class.

when dipped in water, wool yarn swells up,
fabric becomes heavier and stretches,
nylon lights up, paper expands and flakes off,
threads stretch

surfaces in motion

materials

Cloth, light fabrics, pieces of garments, cotton and wool threads; light and porous paper, thin tissue paper, plastic sheets; sheets of plexiglass in different shapes and sizes, and bowls of water.

Manipulating fabrics and papers that have been dipped in water can produce interesting effects of draping and surfaces "in motion", with bulges, pleats, and layers stretching and overlapping. On drying, the materials maintain these altered shapes.

The different composition results vary in relation to the size of the selected surface and the material properties of the fabric or paper used.

By using sheets of transparent plexiglass as support bases and placing them against the light, they can be explored and produce special effects, playing on variations in the transparency and opaqueness of the materials.

procedures

The groups of children at the table had various fabrics, papers, and threads to work with. When the fabrics and papers were still dry, they tried out different situations of surfaces in motion on a plexiglass base. By dipping the selected materials in the bowls of water, they obtained their final "surfaces in motion." The works were then photographed with a digital camera and shown with a video-projector so that they could be seen and discussed by all the children.

An element of variation was introduced in some classes during their workshop activities, with the suggestion that they should use their individual works to produce one large joint composition.

tactile paths

materials

A 10-meter path of materials was laid out on the workshop floor, which was used as if it were a large sheet of paper. The path contained a combination of different materials, forms, and surfaces for the children to explore blindfolded, using their hands and walking barefoot. In this experience, the materials supplied a great variety of visual, tactile, auditory, and evocative stimuli. Some of the materials used in the tactile path were reintroduced in the tactile boxes and in the table activity involving the use of a stethoscope.

polystyrene sheets
metal sheets
pieces of wood
sandpaper
foam rubber
aluminum foil
velvet
tires
steel wool

egg cartons
ceramic tiles
metal sheets
pieces of wood
sandpaper
foam rubber
aluminum foil
velvet
tires
steel wool
ceramic tiles

blindfolded path

*I felt some soft and hard things
and it was great.
At times I felt like I was sinking.*

listening with the stethoscope

metal wire: *I hear a whistling noise.*
plastic: *I hear a thin noise.*
The plastic strips seem like waves.
polystyrene: *I hear a relaxing noise.*
Polystyrene is like a drum.
foam rubber: *I hear a rough noise.*
wood: *Wood is like a storm.*

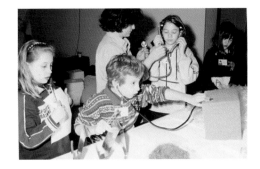

procedures

a

The arrangement of the space consisted of a strip of white fabric laid out on the floor with different white-colored materials placed on top, in a sequence of shapes, sounds, temperature sensations, and surface variations; four tactile boxes (which could only be explored with hands, thus excluding the visual quality of the materials) set on metal bases; and a table with materials that could be listened to with stethoscopes.

b

1. The children explored the tactile path, walking on it barefoot and blindfolded, led along by their classmates holding hands. At this stage, the children were encouraged to listen to the sounds produced by the materials they were walking on. The materials they were manipulating and treading on produced their own spontaneous sounds, but many more sounds could be produced by experimenting with the various possibilities offered by the materials, such as by tapping, stroking, and rubbing them.

2. The aim of the experience with the tactile boxes was for the children to recognize the materials just by feeling them with their hands. The adjectives used and associations made were noted down.

3. The same materials as the ones used in the tactile path were presented through the sound amplification provided by the stethoscope. (By rubbing the stethoscope on the rough surface of the foam rubber or plunging it into the soft transparent ribbon, the noises acquired contrasting and attractive sound qualities).

c

The information station was activated. Cushions to sit on were placed along both sides of the unrolled tactile path. By rotation, the children went around the three "stations" represented by the tactile path, the touch and guess boxes, and the table set up for listening with the stethoscopes, and were able to play with the materials available in each.

d

During the various stages of the workshop, a great deal of attention had to be paid to the verbalizations of children of all age groups. This work of observation and documentation allowed the atelieristas and teachers to make considerations that applied across different age ranges and working areas, and to find the relationships between the children's different approaches to the proposed activities. The practice of taking simple notes of the associations made and sensations perceived can be suggested to the children themselves.

In this case, two children were selected to act as "documenters" of the experience using the digital camera. It was them who eventually showed and discussed the images of the activities as they were being projected onto the wall with the video-projector. When the situation allowed, the documenters also had the opportunity to play around with the materials by putting them through the scanner.

The class was given a workshop folder as a gift, containing two images of the activities they had carried out.

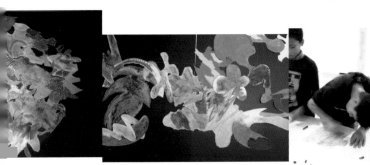
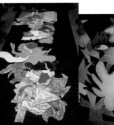

Words mean nothing to me, they talk around my painting. What I want to express appears in my painting.

Matter is nothing but an equivalent of color and, like color, it has its very own weight, essential in the compositional equilibriums and relationships.

The *Gobbi* series originates from a need for experimentation and innovation. I have always felt the need to innovate, to go beyond...

I might be able to obtain that particular shade of brown, but it wouldn't be the same because it wouldn't contain within it all I want it to have.
In burlap, I find that perfect cohesion of shade, matter, and idea which would be impossible to achieve with color alone.

...painting to me is a freedom achieved, constantly consolidated, defended with prudence, to gain strength from in order to paint more.

Alberto Burri

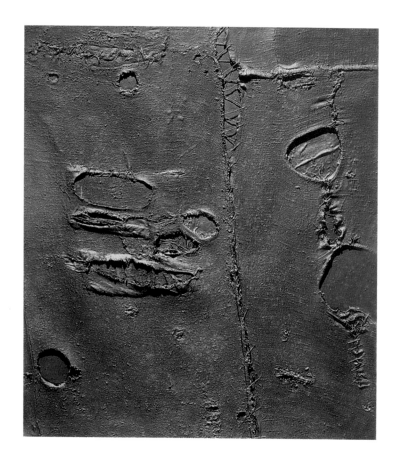

Biographical notes on Alberto Burri

Alberto Burri was born in Città di Castello (province of Perugia) in 1915. He obtained a degree in medicine and, as a medical officer in the War, he was taken prisoner and sent to the Hereford POW camp in Texas.

On his return to Italy in 1946, he settled in Rome, where he dedicated himself to art. His first personal exhibits were held in Rome in 1947 and 1948 (La Margherita Gallery). In 1951, he took part in the establishment of the "Origine" group, together with Balocco, Capogrossi, and Colla, and in the following year he exhibited his *Neri e Muffe* (Blacks and Molds) at the Galleria dell'Obelisco.

From 1950, his *Sacchi* (Burlap bags) started to become an increasingly important part of his work and eventually became a dominant feature in his personal exhibits, which were then being held not only in Rome but also in various American and European cities. From the mid-1950s, his *Legni* (Woods), *Combustioni* (Combustions), and *Ferri* (Metals) started to appear, and the *Plastiche* (Plastics) were added starting in the Sixties. The Seventies saw a progressive reduction in his use of technical and formal media and a greater concentration on the production of monumental pieces ranging from the *Cretti* (earth and acrylic glue) to the *Cellotex* panels (compressed industrial materials). By this time, retrospective historical exhibits of his works were being held all over the world.

Burri subsequently arranged his works in complex cyclical organisms with a polyphonic structure. Examples of this approach include *Il Viaggio* (1979), *Orti* (1980), *Sestante* (1983), and *Annotarsi* (1985 and 1986).

Since 1981, a permanent exhibit of a selection of Burri's works has been housed at Palazzo Albizzini[1] in Città di Castello, as a tribute to Burri by his home town. In 1989, the Palazzo Albizzini Foundation acquired ownership of the former tobacco-drying premises. Under the direction of the artist himself, this complex of industrial storehouses was transformed into a gigantic artwork and the ideal container for his major pictorial cycles of the Eighties and Nineties, which he also donated to his native town. These include the *Matamorfortex* (1992) and *Nero e Oro* (Black and Gold, 1993), and contain suggestions of emerging new themes and ideas which were interrupted by his death in Nice in February 1995.

 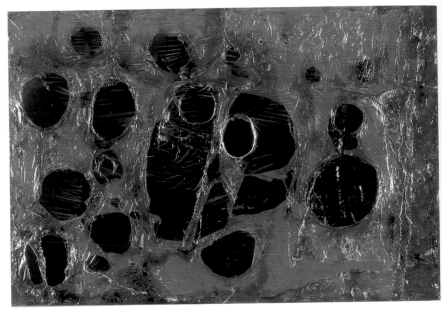

The fortunes of Burri's work in terms of art criticism have been marked, on the one hand, by the reaction-contrast elicited by his work (strictly dependent on the different cultural evolution of the various European and American countries) and, on the other, by more or less definite attempts to fit him into the categories of official art criticism (*art brut*, *art informel*, conceptual art, and so on). Consistent with this logic, the contribution of art criticism from the Fifties onward is an example of a shift in mass taste, from scandalized repulsion, through curious and reasoned acceptance, to today's convinced espousal of his work, in which Burri's role in European twentieth-century culture is granted broad and universal recognition.

Notes

1. The Albizzini Foundation's "Burri Collection," set up by Alberto Burri himself in 1978, houses a rich anthological collection of his works and is the only comprehensive collection of the artist's most significant works. The collection is on permanent display in two venues (Palazzo Albizzini and the former tobacco-drying storehouses) and contains a total of 257 artworks.

from left:

Nero SC3, 1954, 130 x 116 cm
Nero MI, 1989, 151,5 x 202 cm
Rosso plastica M3, 1961, 120 x 180 cm
The images of Burri's works are reproduced from the Catalogue *Burri*, Petruzzi Editore, 2001, by kind permission.

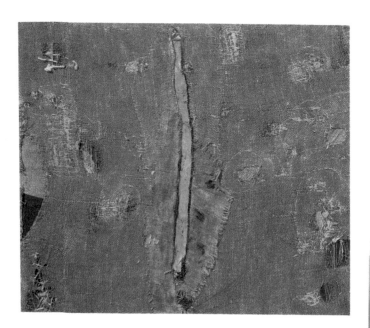

from left to right:

Sacco, 1952, 82 x 100 cm

Images from the Alberto Burri exhibit held at the Chiostri
di San Domenico in Reggio Emilia and exhibit inauguration.

The children's visit to the Alberto Burri exhibit

The paintings felt black to me...

Burri cut, sewed, divided, separated, combined, overlapped, overlaid, and left glimpses.

There's always a bit of mystery in his works, you have to look for things and find them because he used to hide and show things. He made lots and lots of experiments.

He likes colors, like I do. That way, you can create more beautiful works.

We all experience some things that we imagine, different things... No person makes things that are the same.

Burri makes pictures with everyday objects and it becomes fantastic art.

In his pictures there are some things from the imagination and some things from real life.

There's some ashes. He thought it was beautiful. It depends how you look at things.

It was a garbage bag. I think he had some anger inside him and threw it. He was angry and he took it out on the bag.

134

To our eyes, as we looked at Burri's paintings, explored different materials ourselves, and observed the children as they investigated and searched the materials, matter "re-appeared" so fascinating, simple, and mysterious.
Teachers from the infant-toddler centers

Touching with our eyes, we had the sensation of something rough, sticky, greasy, sometimes dirty, because of those smoke stains that also looked like... prints on the sand.
In some of the works, there was something scratching, itching, because of those lines sticking out. Others gave the impression of something very distant in time, like the writing of the ancient Egyptians for example, because of those zigzagging marks. Or some fossils embedded and covered in soil, because of those folds popping out of the painting, or even oil that comes from the center of the earth because of that black color...
Sometimes he would change to create a contrast. In a very dark painting, for example, there was a red streak popping out of a crack that reminded us of lava from a volcano, the heat from food, the pain from a sore throat, red like blood, a heart beating...

Sponsoring the future

Enrico Banfi
Managing Director of Coopbox Europe
at the time of the project, General Manager of Coopsette

Creativity and matter, business and education: how to make a small contribution to sponsoring the future of our society, starting from the end of a construction site and using a cultural event as our underpinning for the occasion.

These were the goals (and restrictions) confronting us as we had to decide "what" to do, in the context of the initiatives arranged for returning the former Sarsa building complex and its new future to the city.

A visit to the Diana Preschool and an interview with its extraordinary "animators," in an atmosphere that is unique for its capacity to grip the visitor's attention and to be overwhelmingly engaging, were sufficient to determine which initiatives – in conjunction with the Alberto Burri exhibit – would be selected to mark the event.

As a business executive who is not emotionally involved through having children or grandchildren in preschool, I felt my morning visit took on an unforeseen course and came to a breath-taking close. By listening and asking questions, but especially by observing and reading the little-big phrases that personalize the Diana School, and becoming absorbed (time just flew!) by the children coming to grips with matter which, in their hands, seemed to acquire an unusual degree of plasticity in terms of both shape and meaning, I discovered an extraordinary similarity between the problems, goals, and flows of modern firms and those experienced in the preschools of Reggio Emilia.

Terms like *project design*, *innovation*, *creativity*, and *plurality of materials* are common to both situations. Valorizing the personality of individuals through teamwork and providing a stimulating environment are goals that the two situations share.

I had read about the teaching philosophies of the Reggio preschools in an American text on management that pointed out how peculiarly effective they are for training managers, among other things. That day, on that particular occasion, I was able to witness this singularity firsthand. I was studying researchers on the other side of the Atlantic, and their points of reference happened to be just next door!

This is how the idea for this educational project was conceived: an idea that we, as a firm, sponsored and closely followed with the same care and attention as the Burri exhibit itself, and even with a slightly greater degree of involvement (and healthy pride in Reggio).

What about the results? Opinions are always subjective. For myself, looking at those artworks (which seems to me to be the appropriate term), I was reminded of the following verses by Walt Whitman:

"There was a child went forth every day,
And the first object he looked upon, that object he became,
And that object became part of him for the day or a certain
part of the day,
Or for many years or stretching cycles of years."

Sponsoring our future starting from children's creativity. This is a simple idea that the Reggio preschools have interpreted in a remarkable way.

Poetic languages as a means to counter violence

Vea Vecchi
Atelierista, Consultant to Reggio Children

"The Expressive Languages of Children, the Artistic Language of Alberto Burri"

When discussing the exhibit that gave rise to this catalogue, it is opportune to clarify the cultural position embraced by the pedagogy of the Reggio Emilia infant-toddler centers and preschools regarding the relationship between children, art, and artists. We have done this every time we have been called upon to reflect on this topic and it is what I shall attempt to do briefly on this occasion, too.

Even when taken separately, the three subjects concerned: children, art, and artists, constitute highly complex topics, and the need to examine them in relationship with one another instinctively increases my desire to skip the problem and cast it aside rather than analyze it.

I almost envy those who talk about it with confidence and certainty. As far as I am concerned, every time I have to deal with the matter, I see it as being so fraught with ambiguity (traditional and historical) that I have a hard time expressing a clear position. I always feel as if I am on some kind of swing that takes me back and forth between divergent and contrasting positions.

I think we should revisit, examine, and discuss some of our previous reflections and positions on the subject in light of different theoretical approaches. However, it may also be opportune and wise to distance ourselves a little from them and continue to regard children, art, and artists as singularities and entities that can yield their best in education only if the relationship between them is considered with the necessary care.

As I say this, I am fully aware that in my work with children over so many years, artistic processes have been crucially important filters for listening and approaching things, and I believe that the poetic languages are among the most important for building a kind of knowledge that can oppose human violence and senselessness. Cognizant of the complexity and sensitivity of the topic, I will therefore limit my contribution to expressing some personal considerations that I have previously discussed in conference papers and writings, updated by a number of recent reflections.

I will start from the children.

To make my reflections clearer, if space allowed me, I would have to describe the processes adopted by the children as they produce their works, on their own or in groups, which the teachers and atelieristas so patiently observe and so carefully document. Indeed, I always illustrate and discuss these processes in my conference presentations, as a necessary prelude to any kind of discussion on this topic.

This documentary material always manages to surprise the audience for the acuteness shown by the children in dealing with the most diverse situations, and also because of the equally diverse and unforeseen (and, at times, unimaginable) solutions that children find to overcome hurdles. It also needs to be emphasized that the historical and cultural situation is constantly changing and we should realize that children and their mental images, their perceptions, theories, and products never remain frozen and unaltered in time, but live and evolve within different contexts. The visual language is conceptual and cultural prior to being formal.

This work of investigation and documentation makes us realize how little we know the children and the strategies they use, and that our knowledge of them has to be constantly expanded, revised, and updated.

It is due to this activity of reflection, interpretation, and discussion about all the precious materials we have gathered over the years that we ask ourselves a great many questions, have doubts, seek exchanges of views, and consider it crucial that the starting point of any of our proposed activities should always come from the children.

We are aware of how easy it is to betray them culturally, however unwittingly. We are equally aware of the fact that being able to "listen" to children and stay by their side in their strategies and mental images, can lead us along paths of knowledge that are utterly original and of enormous epistemological interest.

This way of investigating and working brings back the scent of childhood, with its timeframes, rhythms, wonder, and questions, which we cannot lose sight of if we mean to be teachers, or even simply to inquire into the relationship between children, art, and artists.

Children, Art, Artists

In the late 1960s, introducing an atelier in every municipal infant-toddler center and preschool in Reggio Emilia and a teacher with an art background in the preschools was a brave cultural (and economic) choice, and certainly an unusual one. Then, as now, it represented a strong and tangible statement of the importance attributed to imagination, creativity, expressiveness, and aesthetics in the educational processes of development and knowledge-building.

Gregory Bateson examined very closely the complexity of relationships between the things that surround us. Reflecting on the importance of the aesthetic approach as a major and significant connector of elements of reality, he provided a definition of aesthetics which I feel is so close to my way of thinking and so beautiful, that I would like to quote it verbatim. "By aesthetic," he wrote, "I mean responsive to the pattern which connects."[1] This lucid statement leads me to a consideration that I feel is essential and, in my view, connects the work of artists to that which is done in the ateliers of the schools. I think that artistic thought, in order to be defined as such, must necessarily establish an intense and empathic relationship with things. This approach undoubtedly helps to investigate and highlight the hidden patterns of reality, to create new maps that can combine logical and emotional processes and connect technique with expressiveness: an excellent background for learning as well as a goal to keep constantly alive in schools and in education.

This was the insight, the main idea and driving force behind the comprehensive introduction of the atelier in the preschools and infant-toddler centers of Reggio Emilia, along with the great variety of materials, different techniques, and the process of "thinking" simultaneously with our hands, sensibilities, and brain. The presence of the atelier in schools is seen as a means to safeguard the complexity of the knowledge-building processes, in the aim of using the imagination as a unifying element of the different activities, and of viewing the "aesthetics of knowledge" (Loris Malaguzzi talked about "aesthetic vibration") as "a drive that is rooted within us and leads us to choose between patterns of behavior and thinking, and between visual images."[2]

The ateliers in the municipal schools of Reggio Emilia have chosen the visual language not as a separate discipline, exclusively devoted to the traditional activities specifically related to it, such as drawing, sculpture, painting, and so on. Rather, they have focused on the visual language as a means of inquiry and investigation of the world, to build bridges and relationships between different experiences and languages, and to keep cognitive and expressive processes in close relationship with one another, in constant dialogue with a pedagogical approach that seeks to work on the connections rather than the separation between different fields of knowledge.

We are well aware that any language, in order to be "spoken" and "performed" skillfully, needs to be learned in great depth and in a highly specialized way. We believe this is important and should always be kept in mind. We are equally convinced, however, that a truly cultured language is equipped to interrelate with other languages and has a need to draw from and hold a dialogue with them.

We are conscious of the value of the processes that the visual language can sustain and the contribution it can make to other languages, but also of the fact that the visual language itself can be modified and enriched in turn through a dialogue with the others. These are the links we particularly and consistently focus on in our work and we feel this approach sets us apart from that which the school environment traditionally calls "art education."

Our reasons for being so cautious and culturally diffident in bringing together children and artists in a way that is too clear-cut, simple, and nonchalant are perhaps to be found in these conscious convictions embraced by the pedagogy of Reggio Emilia. In this respect, our position actually reveals a great deal of respect for both children and artists.

There most probably exists a perceptual and representative "alphabet" that is genetically based and inherent to human nature, which constitutes and gives continuity to the links between the first forms of representation by primitive man and contemporary forms, as well as between children and artists from different historical periods. Yet, the environmental and cultural panoramas are different, as are the impulses given to symbols of the basic alphabet and the projection of mental images.

Environmental and cultural differences, as well as age-related ones, should make us wary of correlating too confidently subjects such as children and primitive men or children and various artistic trends, as is often done. It is frequently the case that works created by children are so original, beautiful, full of formal inventions, and poetic, that there is a natural tendency to correlate and compare them with famous artists. However, if we think more deeply about the analogies and relationships between the works of children and those of adult artists, I believe that it could be seriously misleading to limit our search to the formal similarity of the works, which is often purely superficial. Many years ago, I had to explain and justify for the first time the caution shown by the pedagogy of Reggio Emilia when assessing the relationship between children and art, and in defining some of the children's works as art (we have always regarded terms like *creativity* and *imagination* as more appropriate). In my attempt to provide a structured and convincing argument, I was greatly helped by a radical statement by art historian Ernest H. Gombrich. He claimed that it is not art that exists but only artists,[3] that is, men and women who have perceptions, sensibilities, and skills that can transform matter into works of great originality and cultural value, and who have something essential to say to us about ourselves and the world. Regardless of the age-old arguments about the existence of art and its definitions, the "scent of humanity" emanating from the words of Gombrich help me now, as they did then, to structure some of my thoughts on the subject.

The first thing I did was to seek out key words that, to my mind, describe the artists' "processes" as they create their works. Then I went on to assess which analogies and differences may exist between these and the children's "processes" as they do their drawings, sculptures, paintings, and so on. Some of the terms we regard as key words, listed here under no particular order of importance, are *emotional and cognitive tension*, *synthesis*, *innovation*, *courage*, *breaking schemas*, *technical abilities*, *imagination*, *reworking*, and so on. We could continue with this search, but the most interesting thing is that we become immediately aware of the fact that all these processes can be detected in the work of both children and artists. Indeed, we realize that they actually appear in every human being each time a creative act is performed in different fields of activity, although obviously, the culmination of a creative act into a work of art is a rare occurrence.

The specific singularity of children as compared to artists, however, becomes clear as soon as we observe and document (as far as possible) "fragments" of the processes used by the children as they produce their works. The more we look into the strategies they employ to understand and narrate reality, and the more we attempt to "listen" to their points of view (always so surprising to the mental structure of adults), the more we can feel the extent to which their approach to things, their investigations, and their formal and expressive inventions are, in some respects, close to those of adult artists and yet distant from them at the same time. Characteristics such as establishing an empathic relationship with things, keeping the cognitive aspects closely interconnected with the expressive ones, an easy, simultaneous and cross-cutting use of different languages (body language, musical, visual, verbal language and so on), joyfulness and striving to interpret are common to both children and artists. The same applies to their frequent formulations of metaphors and the connections they make between different and unexpected subjects, which is probably attributable to the fact that both children and artists can form mental images that are not enclosed within rigid categories of thought.

What does differentiate children from artists, on the other hand, apart from obvious factors such as technical skills and cultural awareness, is the artists' inclination to show the cleavages, the contradictions, and the hidden side of things, while the children's commitment is to living (and growing up) in worlds that have different timeframes and impulses. I have not included goals among these differences (though it is easy to think they should be) because, ultimately, both children and artists are investigating and questioning reality in order to understand it and are seeking and inventing signs and symbols to represent it.

However, I feel that these correlations and differences between children and artists only have a value, without excessively distorting the identities and paths of each, if we show a great deal of care as we examine their creative processes. Our main task as teachers is to create situations within which these processes can be experimented with, grow, and evolve. This means devising and implementing generative contexts, paying attention to procedures, and creating the right conditions to allow the fruition of the creative process which it is our aim to sustain and stimulate.

The starting point for all these undertakings will always be the child and the group of children, with their mental images and exploratory strategies. This is what we are attempting to do as we observe and document the strategies through which they explore, in an effort to improve our understanding of their knowledge-building and expressive processes, promote the creation of educational situations, and propose activities that are as much as possible in tune with their way of being and, consequently, more capable of generating a high level of participation, interest, and quality.

When I talk about processes, I am fully aware of the ambition inherent in the desire to understand them. Some talk about the impossibility of seeing these processes. However, for a great many years now, we have been conscious of the precious nature of the fragments we are able to capture and document, and of the extent to which they bring us closer to the children, increasing our respect for their intelligences and sensibilities as a result. We appreciate the way these processes make us aware of unique qualities of individuals and groups, of their ways of proceeding and how this can consequently make our proposals more well thought-out, discussed, undoubtedly less certain but, we hope, less liable to betray the children. We agree wholeheartedly with Joseph Brodsky's view when he says that, "when seen from the outside, creativity is the object of fascination or envy; but seen from the inside, it is a constant exercise in uncertainty and a terribly difficult training in insecurity."[4]

We should also take into consideration how the visibility of some of the children's strategies and those of their peers can support their own awareness of their ways of proceeding and understanding. Too often, in didactical approaches to art, artists are considered as the sole generators of creativity, which actually reveals a lack of faith in the creativity of children and young people. The practical result of this is to contradict the very basis of creativity, which requires subjectivity and expressive freedom. This stance, which is fairly widespread, probably derives from a way of assessing the strategies adopted by children while they draw, sculpt, paint, and imagine that is different from ours. Children's encounters with the works of artists will be far more effective and capable of generating creativity if they are given time to investigate and develop their ideas, both individually and with their peers.

We hope that, on the teachers' part, there will be an underlying emphasis on doing a great deal of "listening" to the children's strategies. Without listening, without being responsive to the ideas of others, there can be neither learning nor teaching.

Other aspects which should be emphasized include the wealth of knowledge of and sensibilities toward art which need to form part of the teachers' professional education process. The children's (and teachers') encounter with artistic and poetic languages is a great opportunity and "food" for the mind and the emotions. It is important in education and in the formative processes. This is why we need to prepare the ground to ensure that this encounter takes place in the best possible way. In education, timeframes are long and opportunities need to be recurrent.

I personally believe that the term *art*, as applied to some works made by children's, is not objectionable. Why deny the epithet if the work expresses itself through the creative processes I was referring to earlier? To do so would be a contradiction and

isolate the children's culture once again, while what needs to be done is to reflect in equal measure on the relationships and cleavages between them. In my view, the correlation made by our culture between children's works and art is ambiguous and creates distortions, particularly because our knowledge and mental images of the processes within which children operate is still weak.

Though important studies and reflections have been made on the subject, these need to be constantly updated and, in particular, discussed from different viewpoints. I believe this kind of discussion would bring a wealth of new elements to and develop our own points of view.

New technologies have also introduced new and different elements that are bringing changes to the environment of art and artists as well as that of the children. We need to improve our observation and documentation of the processes that are facilitated and supported by digital tools, as well as the things they deny and alter in relation to traditional tools. We are dealing with a new landscape of possible mental images and technical and inventive action that, as far as children are concerned, is still largely undiscovered. It is a landscape we are in the process of documenting and reflecting upon. Fortunately, in the meantime, the creativity, the mental images, and the cognitive aspects of childhood continue to express themselves and to expand regardless, often overcoming the conformist proposals and requests that a large part of official education (families and institutions) constantly offers to children.

In recent years we have witnessed a growth in the number of places defined as ateliers and workshops (each of us probably has a different mental image of these definitions) which I believe might provide interesting opportunities for children and youth. They are often found outside of school and offer extra-curricular activities. Within school, when they exist at all, they are almost always relegated to a marginal cultural position or form part of optional choices. As such, they are far from fitting the image of the atelier that we have tried to put forward and hope to see, that is, an atelier which is an integral part of the school and a co-protagonist in the processes of knowledge-building and of constructing ways of approaching reality.

The expressive languages of children, the artistic language of Alberto Burri

Recently, philosophy, psychology, and psychoanalysis talk increasingly about a general state of "anesthesia" affecting our sensibilities, and about the separation between the rational and the emotional part of us. They argue that this anesthesia and separation end up producing personality distortions at both the individual and social level. There are many reasons for this, and this is not the place to discuss them. Yet, the reflection is useful to help explain the deeper meaning that guided the didactic project inspired by the works of Alberto Burri.

We believe an encounter between children/young people and poetic languages is increasingly necessary not only for its own sake but also because it can help prepare a fertile human ground where other languages can take root. We believe that of all the different languages, poetic languages have the strongest capacity to maintain a close interconnection between rationality, imagination and sensitivity. Ultimately, they can become the most effective antibodies against violence as well as the most productive means to instill the capacity to listen to others and to the world.

The exhibit dedicated to the work of Alberto Burri (one of the leading figures in the international art scene since the 1950s), held at the Cloisters of San Domenico in Reggio Emilia from November 2001 to January 2002, provided the opportunity for an encounter with these languages. It was an occasion with the power to spark off or cultivate a number of interesting ways of approaching and looking at the world around us.

However, as had happened with other events, the Burri exhibit,

too, ran the risk of "burning itself out" quickly from a possible lack of attention or a fall in the level of interest and curiosity. To fully benefit from such opportunities, we need to ensure that our senses, our curiosity, expectations, and interests are kept constantly active.

The didactic project adopted for this event was based on identifying procedures which would, as far as possible, prepare and vitalize the encounter with Burri's works as well as have the potential for being developed in different occasions and continue beyond the exhibit itself. It was addressed to children from infant-toddler centers through to middle school, and their teachers, based on the belief that the concepts and principles underpinning the work can be explored at any age, albeit by following different procedures.

Something important we sought to avoid was a simulation of Burri's work, as we believe this kind of exercise would be relatively sterile and contrary to the very nature of creativity, which actually requires expressive tension and freedom. In our approach, by contrast, we sought to adopt a stance of attentive "listening" to Burri's works and thus to draw precious suggestions from them which, once suitably redeveloped, could be proposed to the children. We were also concerned that these suggestions should be able to establish a dialogue with the children, based, for example, on the ability to perceive, grasp, and use the chromatic essence of the materials and their identity, to examine the concepts of variation and transformation of matter, and investigate the compositional rhythm inherent in the works.

In our work with the children and teachers, we sought to put into practice and bring vitality into a perceptual and cultural process that would endow elements with a particular identity or singularity by removing them from everyday-ness or from the "indifferent," as Italo Calvino would put it. These singularities then had to be considered in relation to one another. The central object of the project continued to be the child, the child's mental images, strategies, and interests. The focus was particularly centered on the processes set in motion by the children regarding their choice of the materials they meant to use, the identity they attributed to the materials they selected, the dialogue they established with the materials, and the compositional methods they used.

The Alberto Burri Exhibit was an important opportunity to illustrate more explicitly the ideas represented by the ateliers in the municipal schools of Reggio Emilia in terms of the dialogue that can be established between children, teachers, and the poetic world of artists. The work done in the schools and the expressive workshops, conducted alongside and in the same building as the exhibit, became one possible and repeatable research path among many, that involved the relationship between the world of school and the world of art.

We are clearly aware that the path we followed might be strewn with error and ambiguity. Is it possible to establish a dialogue with all artists? The relationship might be more difficult with some than with others, and we believe that in order to undertake such a sensitive didactic exercise a careful choice has to be made based on a high level of awareness of which particular artists, works, and characteristics offer the possibility of establishing an interesting and useful relationship with the children.

The goal we set ourselves with this research experience (as we had done with others) was to "return color and taste, sound and structure to the things of the world."[5] Without an exercised imagination or a tension that allows us to "see" the things we encounter, to renew them (and renew ourselves) through a sense of wonder and the establishment of empathic relationships with the things around us, there is a risk that we may respond to the sensitive world with our senses and mind anesthetized by everyday life. This everyday life can often make people sterile to the pulsing of life and "confuse information with knowledge, common opinion with personal judgment, and

trivial things with fundamental ones."[6] In a world that is in the grip of so much suffering by children, women and men, and where the practice of listening to and showing solidarity towards others often seems forgotten, our response is to re-propose the right to joy and beauty, and to listen sensitively to the things around us. This should not be interpreted as a paradoxical and almost offensive response to the suffering that afflicts so much of the world. Although what we are asking and hoping for, for all children, may appear superfluous or a privilege for the few (joy, beauty, and sensitive listening), we believe it is essential in order to live. It is in this spirit and with these convictions that we work in education. We are grateful to the children and the works they offer us as gifts that express their intelligence and sensitivity, as well as the inherent human need and search for beauty. Our involvement in education is based on our hope for a world in which these qualities are not considered as superfluous items of wealth.

Notes

1. Gregory Bateson, *Mind and Nature: A Necessary Unity*, E. F. Dutton, New York, 1979
2. *The Hundred Languages of Children*, C. Edwards, L. Gandini, G. Forman (Eds.), Published by Ablex, Norwood, NJ, 1993
3. From an interview with Ernest H. Gombrich
4. Joseph Brodsky, *Profilo di Clio* (Profile of Clio), Published by Adelphi, Milan, 1995 – Translator's note: the text quoted here is translated directly from the Italian publication and is not the original
5, 6. James Hillman, *Politica della bellezza* (The Politics of Beauty) Published by Moretti e Vitali, Bergamo, 1999 – Translator's note: the text quoted here is translated directly from the Italian publication and is not the original

When pedagogy and atelier meet

Interview with pedagogistas, teachers, and atelieristas of the Preschools and Infant-toddler Centers - Istituzione of the Municipality of Reggio Emilia

conducted by Claudia Giudici, pedagogista of the Municipal Infant-toddler Centers and Preschools pedagogical coordinating team for six years, consultant to Reggio Children

Interview with

Paola Cavazzoni, pedagogista on the Municipal Infant-toddler Centers and Preschools pedagogical coordinating team for ten years

Lucia Colla, teacher at the Bellelli Infant-toddler Center for twelve years

Daniela Lanzi, pedagogista on the Municipal Infant-toddler Centers and Preschools pedagogical coordinating team for eight years

Lorella Prandi, teacher at the Bergonzi Elementary School for thirteen years

Laura Rubizzi, teacher at the Diana Preschool for twenty-nine years

Mirella Ruozzi, atelierista at the Balducci Preschool for twenty-seven years, currently working with the Gianni Rodari Theater Workshop

Antonio Tinti, teacher at the Balducci Preschool for ten years

Claudia Giudici: The presence of the atelier and the atelierista in the municipal infant-toddler centers and preschools of Reggio Emilia has contributed to constructing their pedagogical identity. This encounter between atelier (atelier and atelierista) and pedagogy has brought changes both to the way in which the atelier was traditionally and culturally conceived, and to traditional approaches to pedagogy. What do you think are the most important changes with respect to tradition?

Mirella Ruozzi: When I began working as an atelierista in the preschools, I'd had experience with expressive workshops, which at the time were quite avant-garde, but the idea was mainly to have children "do something with their hands." I think what is exceptional in the experience of the Reggio Emilia preschools is that this "doing" was never for its own sake, as was the case in my previous workshop experiences, where there was no continuity of processes and we enjoyed nothing more than the pleasure of having "done" something. In the Reggio schools, everything that happened during a project with the children was "collected" by the teachers and atelieristas and reflected upon. This sharing produced ideas for subsequent proposals made to the children. There was a dialogue about how you could formulate the proposal differently. I think this is where there was a significant shift in relation to other pedagogical and atelier experiences, it was precisely to do with this particular way of proceeding according to the "traces" left by the children.

Daniela Lanzi: Reflecting on the significance of the encounter between atelier and pedagogy brings to mind that one of the cornerstones of our educational project is *relationship* and, as we always say, each significant relationship produces changes in the learning of children and adults alike. I believe that the encounter between atelier and pedagogy was the starting point of a wonderful relationship that, as such, has produced enormous changes. Perhaps the most innovative intuition was to create a dialogue between two disciplines that are so different: pedagogy – a formal, technical one with a disciplinary way of thinking –

and art, which brings in creative thinking that confronts things in a versatile and divergent way. Another important aspect, I believe, was not to interpret the atelier as a specific and specialistic place; the dialogue between atelier and pedagogy was possible because neither of them ever stayed enclosed within their designated places: the classroom for pedagogy and the atelier for art. It seems to me that this encounter was fostered by spaces, people, an organization and a way of thinking that did not have circumscribed boundaries.

Lucia Colla: Perhaps this encounter was also fostered by a different idea of pedagogy in relation to the canonical, academic one, the official approach in required readings with an exclusively pedagogical content. In reality, the pedagogy we want to practice is based on an interdisciplinary approach; it takes into account the encounter between different fields of knowledge and this, I think, was reflected also in the encounter with art. The educational background you have as an elementary school teacher, but also after your university studies, often doesn't involve being open to the other fields of knowledge; it doesn't make you think that you may not be self-sufficient. You don't learn, for example, that the expressive languages are really an everyday thing, or how much they are part of the human heritage and of an anthropological approach to knowledge.

Paola Cavazzoni: What Lucia said brought a number of reflections to mind. I think that this hybridization between atelier and pedagogy generated a new idea of pedagogy and a new idea of atelier. The other aspect that seems important is that the atelier brought into the schools an awareness of the presence and the importance of other languages that children have with respect to the ones traditionally dealt with by pedagogy, while our pedagogy made listening to them a possible and everyday practice. In our experience, the atelier was immediately conceived as a place that was non-specialized and part of a wider network and in dialogue with the whole school and center. I think that this encounter between atelier and pedagogy, which suggests many ways of listening on a daily basis, also makes visible the fact that these languages not only exist but are interconnected and ever present in all the aspects of children's learning.

DL: Over the years, this dialogue between pedagogy and atelier has become almost a metaphor for how to work with other disciplines; it has given us a way to approach and dialogue with other "worlds."

Laura Rubizzi: Right from the beginning, thinking about a close relationship between pedagogy and atelier has meant experimenting with the encounter between two "powerful" languages: that of the word, traditionally dominant in schools, and the visual language, closer to the world of art.

In the early years, like today, this relationship had to be invented and constructed by professional figures with different educational backgrounds but with a common idea of children and education. In our experience, the dialogue between atelier and pedagogy is bound to extend to relationships with other languages, continuously renewing itself in ongoing and never-concluded research, able to nurture curiosity and elicit new questions.

CG: Lucia and Paola have underscored the fact that the atelier, right from the beginning, was not specialized, did not relegate the visual languages to one place, but was constructed and defined in relation to the whole school. In this regard, I think that an important moment in our experience was the introduction of the mini-ateliers, a supplementary space inside the traditional classroom that makes it possible for the visual languages to be visible and practicable on a daily basis. This also changed the didactic methods and the organization of work…

MR: This is certainly true, but I think the evolution of the atelier was also aided by the experience of the infant-toddler centers. The teachers there brought in different points of view about young children and their knowledge-building processes, but also in terms of the role of the adult in an educational context.

At the end of the '80s, Vea Vecchi and I did a project on light with the children at the Rodari Infant-toddler Center. Being naturally familiar with the work of various artists of the past as well as contemporary ones helped us to see more clearly what these very young children were doing and to discover that they were "genetically" predisposed to this encounter. Seeing so clearly the intelligence and sensitivity of such young children in relation to an apparently difficult and abstract element like light helped us to modify some of our reflections and behaviors with the older children in preschool as well. In my opinion, in the preschool, the mini-atelier concretely met the need to bring the expressive languages out from the "walls" of the atelier, also because, in the meantime, the teachers had become proficient in offering these opportunities to the children on a daily basis. Then, at a certain point the mini-ateliers also became "too small," because the languages were so many and so interrelated. We had also developed more awareness, for example, with respect to other languages, such as body language. What I like most is when the delegations who visit the Balducci preschool, seeing the classroom of Antonio, who loves dance, say that this, too, is an atelier, because the whole school has to be a school-workshop.

LC: I agree with Mirella: precisely because you have a better knowledge of the children, their potentials, their multifaceted approach to learning, you no longer think that certain interesting things have to be done only in designated spaces and at specific times. It's not enough to have the atelier and the mini-ateliers, because you spend more time focusing on the suggestions you get from the children; you're more able to observe and understand their knowledge-building processes and to construct sensitive contexts that support and nurture them. I think this has been a very strong point for the infant-toddler center: to understand more, as adults, about the children's knowledge-building processes.

PC: What I've sensed more strongly recently is a shift toward conceiving the atelier as one workshop within the workshop of the school. The atelier is like a resonance box that not only emits but also receives sensibilities, attentions, proposals. The other aspect that I wanted to underscore in this encounter between atelier and pedagogy, besides the cultural growth of the school and the didactics, continues to be the fact that it has also had a significant ethical and civil value. When a child enters the school, he is considered also in terms of his differences, a way in which you "can be" in the school that goes beyond your use of words: each child can find his own way of expressing himself, of being and narrating.

LR: I think that the strength of the continuous relationship between atelier and pedagogy is that it has generated a style of thinking that goes beyond the physical nature of the atelier and the classroom and permeates the entire environment and the educational project of our centers and schools. I also wanted to add that, in my opinion, the atelier – giving priority to the expressive languages and documentation – helps to give visibility to the didactics, to the learning processes of children and teachers.

Lorella Prandi: For us, meeting Mirella Ruozzi and Maria Grazia Stefanini [a retired teacher who helped in conducting the project], was an encounter among people more than an encounter between specific competencies. This encounter hinged on a way of doing and thinking that is quite similar, and this enabled us to work together. This project was carried out in these classes because there was a desire to do research and be directly involved, and there was a common language. With respect to what you've said up till now, I like to consider the atelier and pedagogy as places of research, and this is what a school should be. I think school is a place of languages. Going back to the experience of the Burri project, the presence of Mirella and Maria Grazia gave us an opportunity to reflect further, to ask ourselves questions and to develop topics that our school is concerned with: to see how children learn, what relationship they have with knowledge, with the stimuli that you provide, how they relate to each other. We can't say that because there isn't an atelierista at the elementary school, we don't do these projects. Every occasion should be an opportunity for observing the children, to see how they formulate their knowledge, how they establish relationships. I think that certain languages favor relationships more than others. A school must always be in dialogue, and we shouldn't think of these encounters as being only with art but with every discipline. For example, mathematics, too, can be very creative, as can foreign languages.

LC: One characteristic of the Burri project was that it also involved working with the elementary school and the middle school, having shared moments of professional development among ourselves as adults, having encountered each other and prepared the exhibit together. I think these are precious opportunities that design the possible identity of school and of education because they create cultural tension, which I think is generative for the city, for the families, and for the children, quite apart from the specific experience.

LR: As regards the project of the encounter between children and art, in this case inspired by the work of Burri, I think it's crucial to share a theoretical framework and a way of approaching and understanding the artist, forged by teachers, atelieristas, museum personnel, and coordinators together. The project promoted a didactic style that was capable of sustaining the children's creative research, maintaining subtle but deep harmonies, sometimes different, with the creative research of the artist. Perhaps no didactic approach guarantees the creative act, but the approach you choose does make a difference as to whether they can be accomplished or not.

Antonio Tinti: With this project, I think we were able to get a better focus on, share and develop in more depth something that might turn into a slogan and which we risk being interpreted as: "the schools of creativity." But what is creativity? I think it's the ability to make connections and, as Malaguzzi said, to connect the impossible with the possible. An impossible that can be defined as a challenge, asking questions that we often don't know how to answer, for which you need to encounter someone else. Children are the first to make you shift you toward the impossible.

Working with them every day reminds you how ill-equipped you are to recognize what is taking place, to "read" what is happening before of your eyes, in communicating it through the documentation. This is an enormous responsibility carried by the teacher: what instruments, equipment, "backpacks" do you have? What do you put inside them so that listening is an occasion of growth for you as well as for the children, and so that the children build an awareness of learning and knowing?

In the encounter with Burri's poetic language, one of the questions I asked myself was: What is a composition? I became more aware of the relationship between composition, space, and body.

Regarding the documentation of the project we produced (the children's conversations, written notes, photos, videos, and so on), what came to mind was the image of something that descends on one side and rises on the other: if you go into one problem in depth, another one emerges… sometimes it feels like being in a labyrinth. Sometimes these cognitive maps can, and perhaps should, put you off-balance, leaving you with a sense of the "non-finite." This kind of research generates branchings-off, like communicating blood vessels, continuous connective passages from one area to the other, and for children this is normal. The research carried out with the children on what a composition is, made me more conscious of the fact that one material can be space, and one space can be material, and this oriented us in the project with the children.

LP: I wanted to add something about the ability to connect the possible with the impossible. When you encounter the "impossible" of the children, each of us learns something. The children's errors are not errors, but a different way of learning. Just ask the children what they've done and they will it explain it to you. This, I believe, is the construction of knowledge, which takes place by keeping the "impossibles" into account. I like this idea of questioning what "equipment" we have as adults…

CG: Antonio's reflection on the teacher's "equipment" mentioned by Antonio and developed by Lorella brings us to the issue of professional education and development. At this point, I would ask you a question: What were the greatest difficulties you encountered in a project like this one and what supported and helped you? What conditions and strategies?

DL: To me, perhaps, what seemed like difficulties in the project at the beginning were actually its greatest resources from the point of view of my professional growth. There were different aspects that seemed problematic; for example, the relationship between the different levels of school, different realities from many points of view that nevertheless found a way to work together, truly together. Another aspect, to my mind the most significant, is that the working group immediately became an in-depth study group dealing with the research findings as the project progressed. You had to write non-descriptive summaries of the project you were carrying out, then you had to present and discuss them with the group, and that's not an easy thing. Another complex aspect was the presence in the group of young atelieristas who were new to the experience of our infant-toddler centers and preschools. This represented a difficulty due to their lack of experience in working with the children, but at the same time they brought in new points of view, different ideas and interpretations, becoming an enormous resource. Vea, together with those who coordinated the project, had an important role, I feel, in conceiving the project but also in the systematic way and the rigor with which the review meetings were conducted, where we illustrated and discussed our work.

PC: The possibility to work on 0-6 projects has always seemed to me to be a great resource, but here there were new ages involved, children over six years old, and I think this was very important. Many projects bring together different ages, but in this case the idea was not only to bring them together but to arrange for the sharing of ideas between different voices, experiences, roles and generations on the theme of the relationship between children and art, proposing a possible interpretation. Another aspect of professional growth came from

our reflections on the documentation, on giving visibility to the processes of the children and the adults. In this project, listening to the creative processes of the children and the interpretation of the adults always had a significant weight: the adults never took a backstage role but were always very visible and public. The question of "documenting the documenter," that is, how we as adults document, in our work and in our way of being, seems to be a line of research that needs to be developed. We are used to working in groups and seeking dialogue and exchange, which in this project took place between teachers from the infant-toddler center up through middle school, atelieristas with a lot of or very little work experience, and with the pedagogistas. It was an exchange between different roles and professional profiles to construct imaginations and possible future scenarios – that "equipment" we were talking about earlier.

LR: Rather than talking about difficulties, I would talk about strong emotions and questions which I feel I can only partly answer. An emotion still very much alive is that of having participated in and witnessed the creation of material compositions by the children. Children's creativity seems to be driven by the desire and the excitement to continuously discover something new, something to know, or even just to savor the beauty of an image or a gesture that thrills you and elicits admiration and wonder. Their pleasure is at once aesthetic, sensory, perceptual, and emotional. They seem never to want to complete their compositions and when they do, it seems that it's only temporary – the next day they want to continue. How can we interpret the children's research?

LC: The methodological strategies of this group were invaluable, providing new resources and greater awareness for all of us. Another important aspect, I think, was the quality of time. Concentrating the development and elaboration of a project within a set timeframe and sharing rules, is a decisive factor. It creates a cognitive tension that is extremely generative, because you're immersed in processes that are full of curiosity, emotion, and cognitive content, and perhaps this is the condition for our becoming so completely engaged. It was not the first time that we as a center were part of an expanded work group that generates, produces, reflects, and questions. Subsequently, you have to take everything back to your colleagues, so other methodologies and strategies of research are created, other types of exchange, dialogue, and discussion, so time has to be found and "constructed." This project left marks and signs, some very visible, in our center and in the way we now have of confronting other aspects of our work and our way of being with the children. So, even after it was over, the project continued to be very generative, and I think this is what makes a project truly formative. You haven't just opened and closed a project, but you have generated new sensibilities in yourself and in others. I think I can also speak for the parents. The other thing, from the formative point of view, is that it isn't true that , as many other teachers claim, if you open up lots of projects, you end up with a huge workload. In reality we do nothing other than construct contexts and conditions as a possible terrain for further research, for constructing connections and relationships between different kinds of knowledge, that is, a horizontal approach that cuts across different fields of knowledge.

PC: I think we should underscore the aspect of the parents that you mentioned, Lucia. It was a work group that resonated in the experience at the school and center, in a community, where the parents were involved and had a leading role: project presentations, the visit to the Burri exhibit, the visit to the exhibit of projects created in the infant-toddler centers and schools... I think it was an opportunity to revisit some of the values of our experience: the image of the child and creativity, the role of the infant-toddler center and school... It was an important experience, outside and inside the school, and it also elicited new questions about the children. I remember on a number of occasions you could see the parents' incredulity and amazement in discovering that the children were not "older than their years" but they were "old" in their way of being children: "What a lot

of things they know how to think about!"... their humor, their research and explorations... It was also a manifesto of optimism, a message of hope; we saw such wonderful things and someone said to me: "It suggests something good"...

LC: At the beginning, we asked ourselves how to involve the parents, because the other risk is to unwittingly instill the idea of child-as-artist, which is the idea our culture often offers us. Another difficulty was responding to the possible question: "So what's actually the purpose of all this?" There is a need to constantly nurture the parents' reflections and discussions on some of the values of our experience.

DL: I think another interesting thing about this experience was that, in the end, an exhibit was produced that was visible for the whole city. The fact that we had done some nice projects didn't automatically mean that we would also be able to produce a significant exhibit (in fact they involve two different levels of documentation), an exhibit in which you have to think of your work in a different kind of synthesis, to think about *your* work in relation to that of the others. The thought of producing an exhibit also put us under a lot of pressure – there were difficult moments. Mirella, you've always said that for you, as atelieristas, working on the exhibit "The Hundred Languages of Children" was a very important moment of professional growth...

MR: It's true that it was an important occasion of growth but on another level. When we produced the "Hundred Languages" exhibit, we were working on different projects, not a common project for everyone. The difference here is that everyone was working on their own projects which they had to complete but in relation to those of the others. We were working "all for one and one for all" to make the educational project of the schools of Reggio visible. Working to produce an exhibit is certainly an important formative experience, like you said, Daniela, it puts you under a lot of pressure. But these moments of crisis are probably the generative ones, the ones that enable you to better understand the situation.

I wanted to add a consideration on the difficulties we encountered in this project. I had one particular problem. We were asked to work on material with the children, with Burri's works as our point of reference and to provide suggestions. I remembered something that worried me particularly: a long time ago a colleague of mine had worked on Burri, so we went to visit her school. She and the children had burned some plastic, cut up some burlap bags and made these compositions – she had cloned Burri! When the project on Burri was proposed to us, I had this concern. I was concerned mainly for the infant-toddler center and the elementary school, and I asked myself how to offer informal materials without creating a muddle, because in the elementary school there is a very strong culture of figurative art and in infant-toddler centers a culture of "making a mess"! I wondered how to maintain an aesthetic approach to knowledge when faced with the potential risk of falling into the culture of stereotype or of "putting everything together." But a number of things reassured me. First of all, one of the agreements of the project and the structure given to it were designed to prevent this risk; then there were the children, their way of exploring and working. In what actually took place, I rediscovered what Malaguzzi had called "the aesthetic vibration of knowledge."

LC: I believe that what helped us to avoid the risk you mentioned, Mirella, is that right from the start, Vea told us: "Look at the works of Burri while thinking about your children." And we truly tried to look at those works with the eyes of the children. We had to work first of all on ourselves.

CG: The concept of "visibility," of "making visible," has been mentioned several times, and this was achieved through different times, modes, and strategies. What do think was the significance of documentation in this project?

AT: As Lucia and Daniela mentioned, I would underscore the rigor of the process. There were occasions in which you had to communicate what you were doing, narrations that were open every time, but which also had to be incisive – you didn't have to describe everything as if it were all already over and done with, but you had to know how to interpret things in a dynamic way, like presenting a motion-photograph of what you were experiencing; then you had these "X-rays," as if someone was taking a photograph of the conceptual structure of the steps in the process.

LP: I certainly agree with you. It was important to work in a group and to have deadlines. In elementary school, this is essential, because no one asks you anything, it's almost self-management, so having a group with deadlines, a group that makes demands of you, was really crucial! Trying the project out on yourself: this, too, was fundamental.

In the elementary school it was important because we documented a project that then served as a reflection for other groups, we worked inside the school as professional development. In the elementary school, we don't do documentation, no one asks you to document. Indeed, the more you keep things hidden, the less you show them to the parents, the less they can complain, so it's an entirely different logic. Grazia and I really enjoyed having this possibility to document how the children work, and it was a good opportunity at the elementary school.

AT: Knowing how to tell about children's and adults' learning processes in everyday life is still, in my experience, an open question. This experience helped me to really focus in on this self-criticism. Professional development also takes shape in this way, and it's possible only if you are elbow to elbow, teacher and atelierista, roles that are different but contiguous.

PC: For our professional development, it's important to underscore that documentation took place within a diversified process, and a positive thing because of these differences: documentation in different contexts – the school, the infant-toddler center, between schools, in the town – but also through different forms of communication – a documentary, the exhibit, a book, a catalogue. I think this is truly an important formative aspect, also for the new generations. In this project, I believe I also understood more clearly the difference between the concepts you're exploring – variation and matter, for example – and the language you propose and how you document it, how you make it visible and communicable. This relationship between the conceptual aspects and the images and words was not a new thing, but it brought in new research and new awarenesses. And this is perhaps what generated lots of questions also in our colleagues; it elicited a new way of communicating, perhaps in part different from what we have experimented with up till now.

LR: Documentation in progress and on different levels, finally producing the exhibit and now the publication of the catalogue. All this generated interpretive re-readings that shed light on different facets and new understandings. The pulsing of shared moments between different educational contexts, the times of re-elaboration in each school and the identification of different paths, I believe, were what formed the positive alchemy of the final outcome.

The multiplicity of documentation materials also enabled the families to get a glimpse of an uncommon encounter between the children and an art exhibit, but above all it conveyed the emotion of encountering many and diverse creativities and intelligences. The teachers experienced the opportunity to re-signify their thoughts with greater awareness, and learned strategies of documentation and exchange with people from different backgrounds and professional roles, all within a project that was shared, though wide-ranging.

The exhibit and now the book perhaps represent the highest level of relationship and visibility between the cultural project of a city and the educational research of schools.

CG: We began our conversation by looking at the relationship between atelier and pedagogy, and what remained in the background was the relationship between children and art. In your opinion, can art make a contribution to school? And if so, what kind of approach is most consistent with our educational thought?

AT: For us, adults and children, "encountering Burri" was important for putting into focus some images and concepts such as those of the compositional structures that you meet every day, for example, in the graphic language. An encounter that, visiting the exhibit with the children, allowed the possibility – an important one, I believe – to establish a direct, physical relationship with the works displayed also at a child's height. To me it would suffice if the idea began to take hold that even children can encounter works of art and "enter into" them, like one child, Martina B., said: *I went into that picture.* It would suffice to hear people recognize that art has to do with children, because it has to do with humankind – it is man's way of telling about the world. So the effort and the challenge that exhibits pose is a "true" encounter between children and art, through the workshops, an encounter where the children are the protagonists.

For this opportunity and this experience, I feel a strong sense of gratitude, as it was a formative experience certainly for the new teachers but certainly also for those of us who are seemingly more "expert."

DL: I think that art comes into the school anyway, because the children bring it in. I don't know if it always has to be visible like we made it in this experience, because, looking at the Burri material in the schools and centers, I had the sensation – which wasn't entirely clear to me – that the encounter between children and art or artists was an extraordinary act of interpretation on the part of the children, but not an interpretation of the artist; in other words, evocations generated by the encounter with the artist were brought into the daily life of school. If art is an interpretation of reality, then it does come into the school, because children interpret the world in a creative way. In projects like this one, you have to be very careful to respect both the children and the artist, without taking dignity from either one. I think we avoided this risk because we documented and made visible the daily encounter of children with art.

LC: In fact, we didn't propose Burri to the children, but we offered them contexts that allowed them to encounter and explore the concepts of the Burri's poetic language. We didn't have to visit the exhibit with the children first; we went after we had already researched and experimented with children. But I always ask myself: Why are we normally so afraid of this issue? Why do we feel that the encounter between children and art is so delicate?

PC: Also in the theater project, we had to move away from the theater as a clearly-defined and formally recognized place, because the answers were not to be found there, as they were not to be found just in seeing the Burri exhibit. As adults, we had to see Burri, to discuss, develop, and research, but always thinking in relation to the children. In our schools, the choices we make never preclude certain encounters a priori, but we try to understand how and why these encounters can take place in the school and how to ensure that the children and also the teachers are the protagonists of projects and processes. On the other hand, the encounter with an artist, if played only on certain levels, could reveal an overwhelming disparity for those involved and this, like Lucia said, would be a betrayal of the children but also of the artist himself. We need to create encounters and contexts in which the children can be not only executors or spectators, but themselves producers of culture. And this can happen if they are given the opportunity to elaborate interpretations and if, in their search to give meaning to things, they can also produce new meaning.

The job of learning

Tiziana Filippini,
Coordinator - Professional Development Plan, Preschools and Infant-toddler Centers – Istituzione of the Municipality of Reggio Emilia

I am particularly fond of this exhibit, which I believe represents a significant moment in the history of our experience. There are several reasons: the demanding nature of the theme, the responsibility implied by the presence of the atelier in our schools, the ability to bring together different levels of schools and other educational facilities, and for all the reasons expressed by Vea Vecchi in this book regarding the motivations and values of the project.

I truly believe that the project is an important instrument of dialogue, exchange, and for comparing ideas that can contribute to the growth of all those who work in these fields, as it was for those who were directly involved in the project itself.

Choosing to make the children, their creativity and competencies, our starting point, means overturning conceptually and epistemologically the way we conceive education and the role of school, the role of teachers and their professional development.

This project was intentionally designed and organized as an occasion to strengthen the idea of school as a laboratory of listening and field research, from which knowledge can be drawn and reformulated.

It offered us an important opportunity for taking stock once again of our work of observation and documentation, which are indispensable work strategies for sustaining the dialogue between educational action and the learning processes of children and adults.

"Making visible is the art of knowing,"[1] but experience teaches us how difficult it is to see the processes and to make them communicable, even in cases where the encounter between atelier and pedagogy does give rise to effective documentation. Even when we are "fortunate" enough to get close to visibility, we must always keep in mind that what we are looking at is an interpretive narration that needs to be shared and reinterpreted in contexts of exchange between divergent ways of thinking. This is necessary in order to prevent us from assuming that the way we look, hear, and act has a "truth effect," and to improve our ability to relativize our thinking habits.

The possibility of exchange between the different professional competencies involved in the project was highly educational for all. This kind of exchange is not always easy; in fact it is sometimes exhausting, but it is certainly capable of fostering the enrichment, change, and development of our own interpretive theories and conceptual maps, increasing the understanding and broadening the perspective of individuals and the group. The contribution of professional growth is that it not only highlights the importance of reflecting on one's experience but also provides the instruments and procedures for our reflection and action.

The various documentation materials, paper and digital, produced by the individual schools, along with the exhibit itself and this catalogue, became contexts of metacognition with the potential to move us from the level of interpretation to the level of understanding.

Another valuable aspect of the project was the possibility for sharing and discussing issues as the work progressed, allowing us and the children to find our own place within different points of view.

Perhaps the hardest job was to "transgress," to go beyond the appearance and the functional aspects of the material, to look at the most everyday things through a transformational process in which imagination, empathy, and also logic, are equally important ingredients.

It has become increasingly clear to us that the encounter between pedagogy and atelier has meant not only enriching the educational possibilities we are able to provide, but also introducing a new way of looking, helping us to see things in a different way. It has given renewed "strangeness" to that which is over-familiar and stimulated new questions, legitimating an empathic way of looking that maintains and creates relationships, a way of looking that is more accustomed to accepting and urging changes and transformations.

Atelier and pedagogy work side by side in the search for a different conceptual framework for the way we "do education" in school and the way we learn.

The experience of the work we carried out in "The Expressive Languages of Children, the Artistic Language of Alberto Burri" strengthened our conviction that you cannot make good education in school by merely adding options, subjects, and materials; rather, it means adopting an approach that, as Loris Malaguzzi said, qualifies the relationship between children and adults with a knowledge that is at least reliable of the contents and forms of the various disciplinary areas so that they will fuse into a hundred languages and a hundred dialogues.

Note

1. Alfonso Iacono, *L'evento e l'osservatore*, Lubrina, Bergamo 1987

Remida

The Creative Recycling Center

The ReMida Creative Recycling Center was established with the aim to create a relationship between different forces: the worlds of culture, school, and industry, a synergistic encounter that has made it possible to create new resources.

ReMida is a cultural project, a place where the idea is promoted that discard materials are resources. The center collects, displays, and offers alternative and unused materials coming from the remainders and discards of industrial and artisan production to reinvent their use and meaning.

ReMida is a project of the Municipality of Reggio Emilia in conjunction with AGAC (Agency for Energy and Environmental Services), and the center is managed by the international association Friends of Reggio Children.

Each year, ReMida is frequented by over 3000 users from the 300 organizations registered.[1] The center also hosts about 2000 visitors yearly, including teachers, students, scholars, administrators, government officials, environmental specialists, and journalists from various parts of Italy and the world.

Following the opening of centers in the cities of Naples, Chieti, Lecco, and Turin, ReMida has continued its commitment to construct a national and international network of creative recycling centers. New centers will be opened in other Italian cities, as well as in Australia and Denmark.

The aims of this international network are to encourage the exchange of ideas among the centers, design cultural initiatives, share experiences, and organize events, seminars, and conferences.

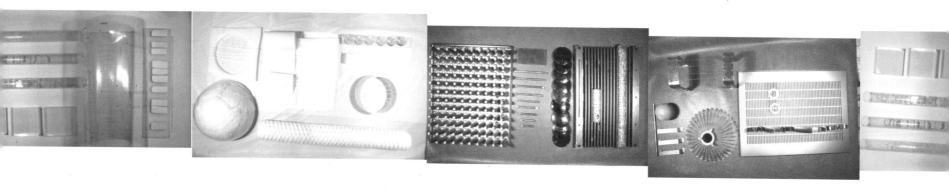

The various organizational aspects include: pedagogical coordination, the coordination of human resources and internal activities, management of relations with the firms that supply materials free of charge, the creative coordination, direct management of the center, the administrative functions, the promotion of educational courses and workshops, the production of informational material, and documentation of the center's activity.

Since May 2000, ReMida has promoted an annual event in Reggio Emilia called "ReMida Day," with projects that promote the materials, creative recycling, and the re-use of materials through various languages (dance, literature, music, cinema, multisensory installations, and so on).

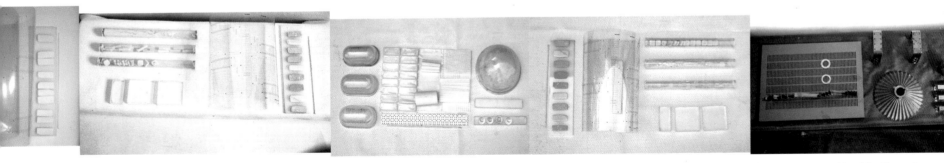

Sound key-board by Alba Ferrari

Note

1. Infant-toddler centers and preschools, elementary schools, middle schools, secondary schools, cultural and sports associations, environmental associations, art studios, play centers, city recreation centers, workshops, church recreation centers, activity centers for the elderly and for youth, centers for the disabled, Territorial Educational Groups (GET), etc.

the authors

Bellelli
Infant-toddler Center

children
from 7 to 28 months old

Alessandro
Alessia C.
Alessia M.
Carlo
Domenico
Elisa
Enrico
Eva
Florinda
Francesca A.
Francesca C.
Giuditta
Iris
Iuri
Ludovica
Maela
Maria Chiara
Maria Grazia
Matteo
Mattia
Michela
Michele
Nazarena
Nicholas
Pietro
Samuele
Sara B.
Sara L.
Simone B.
Simone T.
Stefano
Tamara

Panda
Infant-toddler Center

children
from 8 to 37 months old

Alessandra
Alessia
Carolina
Chiara B.
Chiara D.
Christiana
Edoardo
Federica
Francesco
Giulia
Leonardo
Linda
Lucia
Pietro
Queenly Nana

Balducci
Preschool

children
from 4 to 5 years old

Alessandro
Alessia
Daniel
Diana
Elena
Eleonora
Filomena
Gianluca Francesco
Giulia
Ilaria
Isabella
James
Laura
Luca
Martina B.
Martina G.
Massimiliano
Mattia C.
Mattia P.
Riccardo
Sami
Sara
Stefano
Susanna
Valerio
Vanessa

Choreia
Preschool

children
from 5 to 6 years old

Alessandro
Chiara
Emanuele
Francesca C.
Francesca P.
Gianluca
Giovanni
Giulia F.
Giulia M.
Irene
Jennifer
Laura B.
Laura F.
Luca
Marco
Martina
Matteo D.
Matteo S.
Nicole
Rossella

Diana
Preschool

children
from 3 to 4 years old

Alberto A.
Alberto L.
Alessandro C.
Alessandro M.
Cecilia
Cristian
Daniel
Emanuela
Francesca
Francesco C.
Francesco L.
Giovanni
John
Lisa
Lorenzo
Luca B.
Luca F.
Maicol
Marcello
Marika
Nina
Noemi
Riccardo
Rudi
Valerio

children
from 4 to 5 years old

Anssar
Anthea Ester
Carolina
Cecilia
Claudio
Edoardo Nicolò
Elia
Fabrizio
Fabio
Federica
Federico
Giorgia
Giulia C.
Giulia S.
Hamza
Ibtissam
Jeffrey
Loris
Luana
Luca
Mattia
Pietro
Riccardo
Salma
Sofia

children
from 5 to 6 years old

Alice
Andrea B.
Andrea C.
Andrea D.
Antonietta
Bettina
Chiara
Daniel
Daniele
Davide
Edoardo
Eleonora
Elikem
Emanuele
Federico
Francesco
Giulia
Gloria
Laura
Manuel
Marta
Matteo
Miranda
Oumar
Paolo
Veronica
Vincenzo

Masih Preschool

children
from 4 to 5 years old

Alessandro
Alessia
Andrea
Andrea Lisa
Angelo Augusto
Angelo M.
Angelo S.
Davide
Debora
Emanuele
Federico
Francesca
Gioia
Laura
Lorenzo
Luca
Luce Isioma
Matteo
Michele
Miriam Aba
Simone F.
Simone G.
Sofia
Umberto
Valentina
Xhenifer

Munari Preschool

children
from 5 to 6 years old

Alessandro
Andrea R.
Andrea V.
Camilla
Dari
Davide L.
Davide P.
Edoardo
Federico L.
Federico M.
Francesca
Iman
Jessica
Joshuah
Laura
Lorenzo F.
Lorenzo G.
Mattia
Morgana
Niccolò
Riccardo
Sara
Serena
Simone
Valentina
Valentino

Fiastri Preschool
(Sant'Ilario)

children
from 5 to 6 years old

Alessandra
Alice
Amal
Antonio
Camilla
Elisa
Eliz
Eric
Erica
Fabio
Gabriele
Lorenzo
Luana
Luca
Lucia
Mada
Manuel
Martina
Mattia
Michele
Nicola
Sara C.
Sara G.
Vanessa

Rodari Preschool
(Sant'Ilario)

children
from 4 to 5 years old

Alex
Andrea Be.
Andrea Bo.
Chiara
Cindy
David
Edoardo
Elena
Eleonora
Emanuele
Fatima
Giada
Gianluca
Giorgia B.
Giorgia G.
Giulio
Mareim
Marco
Martina
Melania
Nadine
Nicolò
Roberto
Simone
Valentina

Bergonzi Elementary School

children
from 7 to 9 years old

grade 3 - A
Alessandro
Ali Saad Mohamed
Anna
Chiara
Edoardo
Fabio
Federico
Francesca
Giancarlo
Giorgio
Giulia
Laura
Marco
Marta
Raffaella
Salvatore
Sara
Simone
Svetlana
Ylenia

grade 3 - C
Agnese
Alessandro
Alessia
Andrea C.
Andrea D.
Andrea F.
Claudia
Daniele
David
Davide
Federico
Francesca
Giorgia
Giovanni
Gloria
Grazia
Mario
Marika
Paolo
Rossella
Stefano
Tiziana
Valentina

table of contents